IT'S A SHAME ABOUT RAY

IT'S A SHAME ABOUT RAY

Jonathan Seidler

ALLEN&UNWIN

SYDNEY · MELBOURNE · AUCKLAND · LONDON

First published in 2022

Allen & Unwin
Cammeraygal Country
83 Alexander Street
Crows Nest NSW 2065
Australia
Phone: (61 2) 8425 0100
Email: info@allenandunwin.com
Web: www.allenandunwin.com

Allen & Unwin acknowledges the Traditional Owners of the Country on which we live and work. We pay our respects to all Aboriginal and Torres Strait Islander Elders, past and present.

A catalogue record for this book is available from the National Library of Australia

ISBN 978 1 76106 838 6

Author photograph by Sarah Wilson
Internal design by Bookhouse, Sydney
Set in 13.5/20 pt Granjon Std by Bookhouse, Sydney
Printed and bound in Australia by Griffin Press

10 9 8 7 6 5 4 3 2 1

MIX
Paper from
responsible sources
FSC® C009448

The paper in this book is FSC® certified. FSC® promotes environmentally responsible, socially beneficial and economically viable management of the world's forests.

For Ray, the writer.
And Oma, the reader.

'Yeah, I jumped off a cliff, but let's talk about something else.'

—*Elliott Smith, 1997*

ONE

When Ray dies, we're locked in our house for seven days. We're not allowed to shave, listen to music, go outside or do anything apart from sit mutely in a self-imposed fog of grief, which in Hebrew is called Shiva. We pick through the mounting pile of lasagne other people's aunts keep leaving by the front door.

Shiva is hell for the extrovert. Forty-eight hours in, the four of us are already well on the way to losing it. Our ages span a decade from oldest to youngest; three boys named for ancient Talmudic figures—Jonathan, David, Zac—evenly spaced by two and a half years and dressed identically for much of our childhood, and a baby sister—Zara, named after a Spanish fast fashion brand—whose conception we are assured was not an accident. In addition to being a tight sibling unit who look like babushka doll versions of one another, the four of

1

us are each very loud, opinionated and hyper-social. We're simply not programmed to stare vacantly into space, doing nothing. Eventually Zac, who is studying undergraduate psychology, proposes we watch a stupid movie like *The Fast and the Furious* to get outside of our heads. This escalates into a full escapist saga as we move through the entire *Fast & Furious* franchise, developing quasi-spiritual relationships along the way with Vin Diesel, Michelle Rodriguez and Ludacris. Our family is torn apart by grief but saved from insanity by souped-up cars, hole-riddled plots and a criminally underrated hip-hop soundtrack. The rabbi who comes to counsel us on day three remarks on how well we are all doing, given the circumstances, and we don't have the heart to tell him that while we haven't left the house, things remain extremely high octane in our heads. We're tearing through the illegal street racing worlds of Los Angeles and Tokyo as we live vicariously through another family that rides or dies for one another, no matter what.

Sacred texts are really just stories we tell each other, codified through conversation over thousands of years. In Judaism, the Old Testament is diced up into five segments of real scripture before we bow out and hand over the torch to the new guard. *Fast & Furious* makes it to seven films before the wheels really start to fall off, but even the demise of the group's metaphorical Jesus in *Furious 7* doesn't stop them meting out ever more grandiose biblical battles (see: *F8: The*

Fate of the Furious, 2017). They have their own Midrash meta-commentary too, in the form of *Hobbs & Shaw*, an entirely uncalled for spin-off in which Jason Statham and The Rock—previously mortal enemies—join forces to pummel bad guys and save the world from bioterrorism or whatever.

Evidently, the *Fast & Furious* franchise has all the elements needed to start a religion, including a cyclical collection of parables based around the ancient mores of betrayal, redemption and tank tops for both genders. Vin Diesel's Dominic Toretto is a modern-day Moses, shepherding his flock through one last job before they call it quits and settle in the promised land, which always happens to be one film away.

Naturally, his foil is our blue-eyed, genetically blessed Christ. In July 2013, our dad was no longer alive, but Paul Walker was still with us; our generation's Brando who never got fat or had any memorable lines. *Fast & Furious* is an ensemble deal, and if you study the history—which naturally, I have in some detail—it was actually Diesel who needed to be coaxed into joining what would become the longest continuous car race of his life. But it is Walker who steals the show. He is American exceptionalism on a plate: white, blond, preposterously ripped and somehow able to traverse Black and Hispanic neighbourhoods without attracting any serious suspicion. Paul Walker says what he needs to say with his endless-ocean eyes, which is good because very little of what he says could be considered actual dialogue. Walker spends most of his time on screen as an undercover LAPD cop called Brian O'Conner, who is adopted by the very crime family he is assigned to infiltrate and eventually bring to justice. He is Judas and Messiah both, a perfect deity shimmering against the exhaust fumes of a hotted-up Nissan Skyline under the relentless Californian sun. He is also undeniably the worst policeman in cinematic history.

* * *

By the time we've kicked Shiva, not only have the four of us watched every *Fast & Furious* film currently on the market, but we have also spent hours looking up random facts on Wikipedia about the franchise. We are fully immersed, marvelling at such modern-day miracles as the first film's US$200 million box office haul against a measly budget of $38 million, and the titanic rise of Dwayne Johnson after his franchise debut in *Fast 5*, resulting in him becoming one of the most bankable stars in Hollywood. David confirms another chapter of the *Fast* saga is in production, one in which the crew will apparently return to the United States to avenge the half-sister of a minor character from four films ago. We take bets on the net worth of Vin Diesel—born a very boring Mark Sinclair—and discover he has now amassed more than $220 million. We have holes in our black socks, we have thick beards and unwashed hair, we have stiff knees and sore backs from sitting on the floor, and we are sad that this brief moment in time is over.

* * *

When Ray dies in July, I am technically the only one around, the only one available. Both of my brothers are in Europe, as are my grandparents. My sister, Zara, still a teenager, is in school. The whole thing is incomprehensible, so I do not try to understand it. Instead, I become a grief robot. I book flights. I cancel credit cards. I organise the funeral, wakes, obituaries. I call his friends. I do not cry once, not because it isn't expected of me, but because I don't yet have it in me. I am hard, made of cool marble, impenetrably tough for the first time in my life. I buy an expensive black suit.

It is easy to manage magnitudes when you treat everything as business. I insulate myself against feeling anything by approaching difficult situations with the indifference of a hedge fund manager who could probably lose a million or two just to make a point. I doubt there's a guide to dealing with death that advocates becoming a ruthless ninja, but it helps when faced with hundreds of well-wishers attempting to project their grief onto you, using you as a sounding board to explain how they are coping. If you let even one of these people in then it can easily flood the whole system. So I don't.

In that first week I am always on the move. I answer the phone day and night. I am uncharacteristically unflappable, and people notice. Around day four it becomes clear that the family has started fretting about the fragile, unsustainable state of my mental health. There are heated conversations in other rooms about medication and mood monitoring, but I don't care.

Paul Walker dies in November the same year. That he goes out in an explosive car crash is almost too eerie and brutal to believe, and for months the cast of what will be released eventually as *Furious 7* debate what to do with their half-finished capstone to the holy scripture, and how to give their saviour a fitting send-off. It turns out it was already written. As Dom has relentlessly barked at his crew throughout the franchise, the most important thing in life will always be family, so this film is finished with Walker's uncannily lookalike brothers stepping in to complete his scenes, Walker's face rendered over theirs. It's an uncanny spectacle, bringing the dead back to life through CGI and body doubles. This Paul pastiche is a holy spirit from the next world, reincarnated in his own flesh and blood. To cinemagoers, the experience is nothing short of biblical.

This kind of catharsis is not an option available to me. There is no billion-dollar franchise stumping up funds to augment my father's features onto his surviving next of kin, and it's during the evenings of those first few weeks that this reality starts to become overwhelming. It's too quiet. There's no action. Slowly, surreptitiously, I start to try to siphon out some of the rage generating this excess energy. I've hit the nitrous oxide tank of adrenalin too early. I lie awake in my old bedroom, surrounded by fading posters of Dave Grohl and Chris Cornell, and listen to three particularly aggressive Bombay Bicycle Club songs in a precise sequence. When Jack Steadman screams during the coda of 'Lamplight' I scream with him, roaring so loudly into the dead air of my pillow that all available blood rushes to my temples, threatening to bore a hole through my skull.

Furious 7 is the first *Fast & Furious* instalment I ever see at the cinema. It's almost two years after Dad has died when I settle into my overpriced plush red seat, ready to numb my brain after a long week of work. But the acute problem with knowing an actor in a film has passed, especially when it's a franchise, is that you are hyper-aware someone's had to work overtime to creatively write him out. Characters don't die just because their physical counterparts do. Maybe it works in the franchise's favour that absurd plot arcs are the norm; the last film saw the cast drag racing in Abu Dhabi for reasons mostly unexplained. Nonetheless, it's hard to relax when you're primed for something awful to happen.

The lights go down. Across the theatre, ripples of people prepare to hold their breath for an agonising 140 minutes.

In the end, it's remarkably elegant: a simple metaphor executed cleanly in one long tracking shot to close the film. The accompanying song is pure fucking schmaltz, the kind that circles back around for one more obnoxiously soaring chorus right when you thought there couldn't possibly be any more gas in the tank. 'It's been a lo-ong day, without you,

7

my friend,' warbles Charlie Puth as the camera pulls back reverentially on two cars racing alone on an endless highway, 'and I'll tell you all about it when I see you again.' They're rocketing along, Dom and Brian, Moses and Jesus, black Dodge Charger and a gleaming white Toyota Supra. The significance doesn't really click until the drums blast back in, and out of nowhere the road ahead suddenly splits in two.

Dom drives on. Brian drives away.

In the enforced darkness of the multiplex, the weight of it all finally hits the grief robot, and he sparks, blows a fuse and totally falls apart.

The scene continues on for what appears to be an eternity, Dom and Brian getting further apart until eventually, mercilessly, he veers off-screen and out of our lives forever. I am a mess. It feels so good to cry that I can't stop, even though I'm afraid I'll embarrass myself in front of my friends and this packed-out cinema. I look around, matted eyelashes futile windscreen wipers for the torrent gushing from my eyes. Everyone is bawling.

'It might be the best moment in cinematic history,' Vin Diesel says later of the scene. 'Men around the world—everyone was able to cry—but men around the planet, for the first time in history, were able to cry together.'

He's right. I miss Paul Walker. But really, I miss my dad.

TWO

There is absolutely nothing normal about the Eastern Suburbs of Sydney, where I grew up. The sooner that's cleared up, the better.

There is an embarrassment of water where our family mostly still lives, the pointy end of The East where the tree-lined streets are huge and winding and the houses can be seen from space. In minutes, two parallel arteries can connect you to our San Pellegrino–sparkling harbour or multiple world-class beaches, both of which are warm and clear enough to swim in for ten months of the year.

Sydney is far bigger than this, of course, but this is not a story about the rest of Sydney. This is a story about the select few suburbs that make up the fairytale apex of The East, the ones with garages that have better views than most apartments, where kids grow up knowing that secret access to a shoreline is only a few steps from their front door. The swimming isn't everything, but it says a lot. Many Sydneysiders have access to a body of water; ours is a city unfairly blessed with more than 100 saltwater spots in which we can submerge our bodies after sizzling our skin. But only in The East— which, again, is absolutely not normal—is there truly this much of it.

Aside from the varying shades of blue-green that surround it, The East is defined primarily by insane levels of wealth, much of which has been amassed by people who managed to escape one of the most unimaginable atrocities in modern history. The East is where Holocaust survivors are recast as billionaires, their children go on to become property moguls, and their grandchildren—my generation—buoyed by two generations of staggering success and prosperity, and having never known starvation, work camps, the separating of women and children at Auschwitz and Treblinka, the empty shoes on the Danube, the death marches, the gold crowns extracted from corpses, the near-obliteration of everything, instead become seemingly invincible.

The Eastern Suburbs of the nineties and beyond is a gleaming, linen-clad middle finger to the Nazis. It's *The OC* where every character is Seth Cohen on a protein-rich diet; confident, attractive, rich, insulated. Magnificent, sprawling day schools comprised only of Jews whose parents buy them matching black Volkswagen Golfs when they turn sixteen, who celebrate their freedom to practise religion so aggressively that many never meet or date outside of their lane until they hit university, and certainly never move beyond the invisible Eruv, that religious enclosure of The East. They put down deposits on million-dollar apartments with a little help from their grandparents, who arrived here with nothing when Bondi Beach was a criminal backwater, a sewage outlet, before they banished the shit way off into the ocean so they could forget the smell of human waste, even if they have never forgotten the smell of human flesh at the crematoria, their progeny visiting in fleets of automobiles once championed by Hitler to celebrate their miraculous eighth, ninth or tenth decades on Earth.

Still kicking into their nineties, both my grandmothers are survivors of different stripes: Nana from Siberia, Oma from Austria, each surrounded by death as teenagers, then crossing the equator by sea as near-orphans. The land where they settled has become one of the largest collections of these survivor miracles outside of the Holy Land. The extreme East in Sydney is where The Happiest Man on Earth, Eddie Jaku, beat Buchenwald and lived to reach 101; where history isn't just relayed anecdotally to the young but still breathes alongside them. There's pretty much nowhere left on the planet, certainly not with this level of prosperity or harbour views, where people who lived through such a monumental event can be wheeled out to slap down the naysayers with a simple 'I was there.'

The East where our ancestors settled is a trick mirror, a place where you can grow up in a multi-storey house with a large pool and still consider yourself only moderately well off. It's a catchment area where having a boat is expected, a dock attached to your property is not unusual, and travelling to Europe on a superyacht with kosher catering somehow makes sense.

* * *

I am, in later years, increasingly embarrassed of where and how I have grown up. It feels deeply disingenuous to eke out some claim to tragedy, personal or otherwise, when my adolescence was spent getting wasted in marble-floored mansions and making out on tennis courts that overlooked a harbour most of Sydney's residents only glimpse on special occasions. This conscience crisis probably happens to kids in other wealthy enclaves built off the back of ethnic migration, but our East has a particular reputation as a funhouse of shame, where the risk of appearing weak before your peers is buttressed by an intense desire not to let your forebears down. These social pressures are not an imagined issue, either. In addition to building a Jewish microstate from the rubble of a world war—a mini-Israel that's properly functional, and arguably safer—the people of The East, so far from being driven into the sea by their enemies that they actually live atop it, have built a world of surveillance.

Everybody there knows everyone's business: who is cheating on their husband, who is flunking Year Eight maths, who just got work done, who has bowel cancer, who ripped off their own cousins, who made a killing on the market, who is seeing a therapist, who just came into money, who just lost it, who got cold feet at the Chuppah, who isn't giving to Israel, who is giving too much, who leans left, who's too far right, who is cosying up to the new rabbi, whose daughter has an eating disorder, whose son smokes cigarettes in the park after school, who just changed synagogues, who has stock tips, who had a miscarriage, who gave their son the same name as their best friend, who is about to come out, who will never come out, who is in the private security group, who is dating a goy, who has a weapons licence, who is eloping with a shiksa, who is a convert, who comes from a reform family, who has dementia, who is chronically depressed, whose family gets handouts, whose partner is into weird sex stuff, who just broke another heart, who gets discounts at the kosher butcher . . .

You don't need to know all of this, but if you don't have a sense of what it's really like to live in The East—a place of unimaginable splendour and anxious proximity—where you can live in a house so big it needs three different internet routers but where judgement seeps through the walls, this story might hit different. Because surveillance and shame are

Siamese twins: even if you separate them surgically they'll always belong together.

Having sprung up from ancestors who rightly believed their entire continent was dangerously obsessed with them, the people of the Far Eastern Suburbs, these proto-Jews like myself, have grown up believing that everyone cares about them at all times, resulting in a truly bonkers public–private panopticon where nothing is a secret but we all labour under the pretence that it is. That includes any number of facts about me, chief among them that I grew up with money, went to a private school, and that my father did in fact suicide in a two-storey house with three internet routers and a very large pool.

* * *

Dad had significant mental health issues for most of my life, and none of us dared ever breathe a word about it. Adding to the complexity was his choice of career; until very recently, doctors diagnosed with clinical depression or other such ailments were considered unfit to practise, so in addition to losing face in the community, we also faced the very real threat of losing our household income. Shame, then, was everywhere: a mutation of the shame my Opa, Oma, Nana and Grandpa were made to feel simply for existing in Nazi-occupied Europe, recurring further down the line in strange configurations, like food allergies inherited from the starvation generation.

With very few exceptions, we didn't talk about what was eating Dad while he was alive, and that shame continued after death for many years, until Mum finally sold the big house, the one with the blue roof, push-code front gate and kitchen with a granite breakfast bar overlooking a golf course. I loved my life back then, and continue to be grateful for it, but it was implicitly understood that we lived under sun-drenched surveillance—it was something drilled into us and all of our friends from an early age; the community knew everyone's business, and were naturally smacking their lips, salivating at the possibility of chewing through the gristle of ours.

This complex sensation gnawed at us all in the immediate aftermath of Dad's death. After years of practice we never had to properly discuss what we wouldn't discuss. We simply sat shellshocked in the splendiferous house that would soon belong to another family just like ours but sans tragedy, blue tiles and green grass, full fridges and savings accounts, and informed a steady stream of visitors—those hawks in doves' clothing filling our 1.4 kilometre street with luxury cars and the lingering funk of smoked salmon—that at 61 years old, in apparently rude health, Ray had just 'suddenly died'.

THREE

To some extent, we all live in the shadow of our parents. As they age and we have children of our own, we wrestle with their legacy, try to reclaim some of it for ourselves. The scenes switch and we become somebody's father instead of just somebody's son; family always, but now standing that much taller, our own shadows taking longer to taper off.

The problem with Dad was that because of the nature of his death, his shadow never receded. After he died, his existence took on a life of its own and blanketed us for years. It stretched and rippled out in every direction, casting a fog over the thousands of people who loved and relied upon him as a doctor, advocate and friend: from Kings Cross, Sydney's original Sin City, where a brushed-metal plaque bears his name; across suburbs and seas; and finally, into his family home, where we remained in flux, nobody's father, and suddenly, without warning, nobody's sons, daughter or wife.

Ray's life was wild and rich, stuffed to the gills with complex characters. Spinning yarns was something he did effortlessly well, his photographic memory the bedrock of a rollicking memoir. Combine Dad's penchant for embellishment, the kind where cops suddenly become chief sergeants or two-bit junkies are recast as crime bosses, and you've got a bestseller on your hands. A life lived mostly anecdotally is surely one worth retelling. He should have been the one to write the book.

I've got a lot of things in me, but so many come from him that sometimes I feel like a rough sketch of a much more complex work—a single, trapped, static cel from a complete animation, like the framed Betty Boop that used to hang in our kitchen. The likeness between us doesn't stop at the photos of him as a teenager, which are uncannily similar to me at the same age. It's in mannerisms and the tics, the need to please and the quickness to anger, the nervous drumming and sudden singing, the way we hold a room with exuberant, rapid-fire storytelling that is, at best, always only around 70 per cent truth. Fill in the colours, those deep reds and stunning blues around my stark black Sharpie edges, and stand back. It's not clear who you're looking at anymore.

* * *

Dad was very proscriptive about sugar when I was growing up. Mum too. It was the early nineties and Australian parents were finally waking up to the idea that the lucky country had also somehow become one of the fattest while nobody was looking. By the mid-noughties, our fast-food addiction helped us overtake the US as the world's most obese nation per capita, with 26 per cent of our population dangerously overweight, a problem that took root in the decade I came of age. Exceptionally health-conscious, my parents weren't about to let us take a hit from the 'fat bomb' threatening our generation's future. There were no chips or chocolate in our lunch bags. Our afternoon snacks were vegetables, and after-dinner treats were plastic plates piled high with fruit. Suffering from a lifelong addiction to the sugar rush of Coca-Cola, Mum had also banned all fizzy drinks from the house. We were only allowed supermarket home-brand apple juice, which Dad would pour scientifically from the two litre bottle before filling up the remainder of our glasses with tap water. This is all I knew of juice for ten years.

Later, I learned the word for this. Dilution.

I loved words from the moment I met them—a family trait. The more I collected, the bigger and more powerful I felt. I read faster than I could understand, faster even than I could speak, and lurched into adolescence with a formidable vocabulary I didn't entirely know how to use, one full of words I still often don't know how to pronounce. It's entirely possible that you will encounter words in this book to which I have ascribed a different meaning than their correct dictionary definition. Having access to many words is a gift, a truly wonderful thing, even if you're not totally sure what you're doing with them. But unless you're someone as preternaturally gifted as Ray, who truly talked the talk, I've found this sort of verbosity usually results in a dilution of meaning. Language is all we have, but it has a way of getting in the way.

In my previous line of work as a music journalist, I was lucky enough to meet many songwriters who deliberately messed with the meaning of words, experimenting with the boundaries of language to form unique cadences. Having sat down with people like Daniel Johns and Tim Rogers, I learned that you could be wrong on a page, but you were never truly wrong in song.

This marvel of subjectivity probably goes some way to explaining my lifelong obsession with music. It's all in the delivery. Charisma can transform questionable rhyming structure into magic, no better demonstrated than if you read pretty much any of the lyrics written by Paul Banks of New York post-punk indie band Interpol—a band I once tried to skip my English finals to see live in concert—sans context:

It's the smiling on the package
It's the faces in the sand
It's the thought that moves you upwards

Embracing me with two hands
Right will take you places
Yeah, maybe to the beach
When your friends, they do come crying
Tell them now your pleasure's set upon slow release

The song is called 'Evil'. When you hear it, you'll know what I mean by this interlocking pleasure-zone of words and music. That's the dimension I step into when Banks lands on those precise, utterly nonsensical lyrics, and sets them against the indelible, swaggering bass of Carlos D, his staccato syllables facing off against Sam Fogarino's relentless syncopated snare. Say those words and they mean nothing; sing them and they are everything.

* * *

My siblings still love to test me on how to properly say words, even though we are now adults. 'Huawei'. 'Giuliani'. 'Fauna'. 'Hyperbole'. It's Zac's and Zara's favourite game to play around the dinner table. They clap their hands over their mouths with glee whenever I get something wrong, which is frequently. I understand. There is something novel about a professional writer who can't really say the things he means.

By definition, conception is a process of dilution. Mothers and fathers enter the equation and change the formula. In our family, the measurements were off. The concentrate, which started with my grandfather Marcell, a manic-depressive ball of exuberance and sexual energy that very nearly derailed Dad's life but instead continued through Dad and down into me. Substitute languages, backgrounds and environments and you're still left with the strong stuff; hairy, wiry men with strong feelings, opinions and eyebrows. I don't just look the same—identical, even—to Ray and Marcell. I often feel it.

I tasted pure apple juice at a birthday party in a local park when I was eleven, around the same time I had my first gateway sip of Sprite. The sensation was immediate, overwhelming. I didn't know how to process it; the rush of sugar and bubbles made me berserk. It was too much. I ran around the grass like a lunatic until eventually I threw up.

Madness poured from my grandfather, a displaced child of war and classic old-world Austrian who knew how to dance and ski so elegantly and then one day blinked and found himself at the arse-end of the world. Two generations later it's in me and I'm trying for a baby, the lone survivor of an illness that's stalked the firstborn men of my family for decades and that I'm statistically most likely to pass down, along with an arsenal of words I can arrange but not enunciate properly.

The undiluted version.

* * *

I was about 22, sitting on our front balcony in the sun, when the buzzer went. Two pale, stone-faced men appeared in the doorway and asked me if I wanted to have a chat. I've since learned that nothing good ever comes of this question. If I was smarter I probably would have jumped.

A few years prior, something had gone wrong with me in my very first semester of university, and nobody could figure out how to fix it. I began having anxiety attacks, panicking. Soon I'd stop sleeping for days at a time, eventually having to defer or wipe out of exams that were usually my forte. I withdrew from classes, cancelled all my obligations and retreated to my room. Someone had decreased my colour saturation down to zero; I was completely listless and silently hated everything about myself. This anhedonia had arrived seemingly overnight and was very worrying to my parents. I was prescribed Zoloft, a mild SSRI, by a religious Jewish GP who took notes on my trichotillomania, a new habit of uncontrollably pulling out hair from my scalp and brows. I stared at the floor, saying nothing.

By the time of the balcony incident, I had been put on and taken off almost every drug available, from antipsychotics to tranquillisers, Ativan to Zyprexa. I pinged across the psychological spectrum until someone very important with lots of fancy letters after his name finally got to the bottom of it and handed me a newly diagnosed personality scribbled on a piece of paper, but not before the intense combination of uppers and downers tripped me over into my first taste of mania and I became unrecognisable to my family.

Of my many new habits, the chief concern was my smoking indoors. It wasn't a good look for a doctor's son to have taken up a habit that the rest of the country was rapidly doing away with. I wish it had ended there. But I also brought home young women I didn't ever recall meeting, and got behind the wheel of my car while on stupidly dangerous amounts of illegal substances. I came up with a ludicrous new business idea every day, sometimes every hour, and then yelled hysterically at my parents and friends when they wouldn't back it. I often neglected to take my meds, or took them all at once. One night at 3 a.m., fiending for cocaine and unable to secure any, I crushed up a magnesium pill and snorted it, which nearly destroyed my nasal cavity. For the first time in my life I gained serious weight, and I wrote highly inflammatory articles for publications that have since mercifully gone out of circulation.

I was amazing, all the time. Everyone else couldn't keep up.

The two Vanilla Ice henchmen in the doorway represented the end of the line. They were from the Mental Health Crisis team and had come to figuratively and almost quite literally talk me off a ledge. B1 and B2 politely informed me that I was to take my prescribed dosages in full view of my parents from now on, or I would be scheduled. This is fancy medical talk for being locked up. I'd seen glimpses of what one of these institutions was like. Dad and I had walked past them a few times on our way to the hospital when he visited patients. There were always men wandering in a stupor near the security doors, wearing tattered clothes that didn't fit, searching for cigarette butts. It was where the unreality of being Super Mario with unlimited lives met the reality of being mad. Having spent enough time in the thrall of medicated depression, I was not enamoured with the idea.

It dawned on me that my family was afraid of me. Dad had essentially called the thought police on his own son. My brothers were keeping their distance behind the glass in the living room, gaping at the unravelling scene. Mum stood nervously behind the men, using them as some kind of mock human shield. A house full of emotionally intelligent people, completely out of options.

I didn't remember it getting this bad. In fact, I didn't remember anything.

All fathers want their sons to be a bit like them. There are probably also attributes they'd rather not be handed on. This is my only rationale for why Dad allowed me to be stuck in emotional pinball for years when he probably already knew the answer to my new problem—or at least how to find someone who did. What must it have been like to realise that an undetectable infection that has plagued you since at least the 1960s has secretly slithered its way into your kid's genetic material? You can't test for it, or head it off at the pass. You simply wake up one day to a child transformed.

The erratic behaviour on display in our house was highly unusual to the rest of my family, but wouldn't have been news to Dad. After all, he'd grown up around someone just like me.

FOUR

He is walking with his father and it is not a walk he wants to be on. The fresh air is insulting, there's too much light, the greenery is oppressive. He wants to be in bed, coiled tighter and tighter under the covers until he is nothing.

There is an unspoken roster shared between the son's two younger brothers and his parents. Despite the dimness, he is aware of it. If it were to be the sort of thing that you would stick on the fridge, like a list of cleaning chores or whose turn it is to take the bins out, it would be titled Get the Eldest out of Bed.

Today it is his father's turn. They are walking slowly, his father asking all the questions the books have taught him are necessary. His father hates this job. He would gladly trade it in for taking out the bins for eternity. Spending time with his entirely serotonin-depleted son is excruciating because the father and son are the same. Not just in blood, or in appearance, but in disease.

Death of the firstborn is the final plague God sends down to the Egyptians after Pharoah refuses to let Moses' people go. Moses, this father's Hebrew name, is experiencing the spiritual and emotional death of his oldest son. Seeing these two is looking at and through a mirror, observing the same invisible coding gone bad.

The son is what happens after the dust settles. Softly spoken, downward-looking proof of the curse of faulty genes. Top of the class to bottom of the barrel, effervescent to extinguished, two spirits unrecognisable to one another. He is a cocktail that has become stronger with every shake, infusing the madness of his grandfather and the sadness of his father. He thinks about this relentlessly, this plague. When you are depressed there is nothing else to think about except the inevitability of terrible things.

'Honestly, sometimes I wish I could just kill myself and be done with it.'

It is the first time the son has spoken in an hour.

'I can't stand feeling like this.'

The father is furious. He's known for sudden flare-ups in temper, slamming doors and harrumphing down the hall, but the son has never seen him switch this quickly.

He grabs the son by both wrists. 'Listen. To. Me.' His speech a low hiss, punctuated by spittle. 'Don't ever say that again, you understand me?' It looks like he might cry.

The son, prone to blubbering at the slightest provocation, already is. They stand on the side of their street, locked in an existential battle. One car toots another in the distance.

'It's a sin. A sin. You know what happens to Jews who kill themselves? They don't get buried in our cemeteries. They are nothing. Nothing. Do you want to be nothing?'

He lets go of the son's arms, pacing back and forth near the tree. In the decades to come, the son will remember this moment with crystal clarity. This is the same street the taxi will drop him to when he discovers his father has taken his own life.

'This will pass. You need to trust me. It will.'

'It won't, Dad. This is who I am going to be forever.'

'You don't remember, but I do,' the father says from beneath the dark cover of the ficus. 'This happened to you two years ago. It will pass. You need to do what Jeffrey told you, to intercept your thoughts before they settle.'

'I hate myself. I hate myself so much. I don't want to be here.'

This is more conversation than the son has had with anyone in weeks, and he's shaking with the effort.

It only enrages the father more. 'You are so lucky. You have no idea how lucky you are. Are you walking with two legs? Do you have cancer? Are all of your grandparents alive? Look at the house we live in. Look at where you went to school . . .' He trails off. The son is gone, he can sense it. The flower has folded inwards; though the son is still there, walking slightly behind, the haze has consumed him again.

'Don't ever talk about that again,' the father says quietly. 'Promise me. It's a sin, do you hear me?'

FIVE

I first hear it at a house party.

It's that liquid dusk era of adolescence where cliques coalesce quickly at social events. Binge drinkers on the balcony, smokers in the backyard, and in the parents' home office the early adopters are figuring out how to fashion a bong from a Gatorade bottle. And here in the bedroom, where the only functioning hi-fi system is, are the rockers.

I'm not sure yet if I'm a rocker. I have one foot in two camps, seeing what the girls gravitate towards. Always the crowd-pleaser, I'm trying on 50 Cent for size one minute, skipping over to Red Hot Chili Peppers the next.

But the evidence is mounting. I play the drums, am in a band, gel my hair in spiky tips and write secret poems about dying. Doomed to be a teen rocker, though I don't know it yet. In the dank room that smells too much like Lynx Africa there's a minor squabble before one of my friends emerges victorious, slipping a shiny new burnt disc from his battered black CD wallet and jamming it into the system.

* * *

In the ensuing decades, it will not be a strong look to admit that I had a life-altering experience listening to a single Linkin Park mp3 ripped straight from the bowels of the internet. Nu-metal, the divisive musical genre this group perfected to the tune of multi-platinum sales across the world, is and always has been persona non grata for serious culture heads. It's juvenile. It's reductive. It's often misogynistic. But right there in a middle-class suburb wrapped around two golf courses, in my thirteenth year on Earth, I absolutely, instantly fucking *loved* it.

The song was 'Papercut' and it was the loudest, most propulsive thing I'd ever had smashed through my teenage ears. It's music that consumes and obliviates, firing on all cylinders as it maxes out within the first five seconds and never lets up. There is no God for Linkin Park, no sanctity, no rules. Their work is a dangerously over-packed blender of electronic and rap and heavy metal and pop. There is so much sound stuffed into just this one song that it almost defies belief. That indelible evening, I kept staring through the dark and weed smoke at the blue plastic hi-fi system, waiting for it to catch fire and melt.

Linkin Park officially has two vocalists, but in this forma-tive moment only one mattered to me: Chester Bennington. His singing sounded more like screaming; a writhing, venomous snake uncoiling itself from within his diaphragm and darting out from his larynx. His pain rolled as deep as lava, and I could feel it, more than anything I'd felt in my very limited life.

Chester made the tiny hairs on the inside of my eardrum quiver. It seemed to me as though he was throwing his body against the wall with every note. He was shouting, screeching, singing, snarling, then sucking up all of the oxygen and starting again. His capacity to do this seemed infinite. He was hurting; he was hurting himself, and though there wasn't yet anything in my life to match this pain, I was drawn to it. It was mouth-watering, it was raw, and as I sat cross-legged on my best friend's bed, watching the rockers headbang around the room in saggy jeans, I was overcome with a hunger for more of it, all the time. I wanted to eat this anger, eat it until I was beyond full, until I was bloated, belching and retching fire.

* * *

I do the only sensible thing: go home, steal a credit card from Dad's wallet and sign up online for the Linkin Park fan club. It's only US$30, but I am not yet aware of the twin devils that are Terms and Conditions. When Ray storms in one evening to ask if I know who's charged him 500 bucks in foreign currency, it doesn't help that I'm wearing the band's thick black Gildan band t-shirt that's two sizes too big, and blasting their album at full tilt.

He'd be furious either way. But as it turns out, he really dislikes this kind of music.

'What is this garbage?' he asks, snatching the pristine jewel case from my hands and reading the track listing on the back. '"Crawling". "Runaway". "By Myself". "In the End" . . .'

I don't answer. Refusal is all I have. It's in my code of conduct. It is allowed. It is expected.

'Jesus,' he says, aggressively turning down the volume. 'Talk about music to slit your wrists by.'

It takes Dad three emails and two heated international calls to cancel my membership. I am unofficially grounded, and spend the summer working shifts at his surgery to pay back the bill. But the rabbit is out of the hat, and he nor I can stuff it back in. I have quickly discovered them all, drawing a line backwards in a flurry of proto–search engine pre-Wikipedia research: Nirvana, Soundgarden, System of a Down, Queens of the Stone Age, Korn, Tool, Metallica, Marilyn Manson, Nine Inch Nails.

My head and heart are filled with black bleakness in this perennially sun-drenched city. It is delicious, and I am starving.

An entire universe of music to slit your wrists by.

SIX

Ray runs away.

He runs to escape himself, slipping away just as the sun begins to peer over the glistening dew of the back lawn, sliding through the side exit, past frangipanis, blooming November lilies and hydrangea, closing the gate with a painstakingly delicate click. His black sedan backs out of the garage, and behind the steering wheel, as the car rockets down the empty dawn road, he finally relaxes. He's made it.

The family sleeps, children strewn across two levels, his wife right beside a warm patch that still radiates heat when she jolts to and realises at once that it's happening again.

When Ray runs away he never says goodbye. He drives on autopilot, not caring where he ends up as long as it isn't where he was. Later, in psych sessions, he'll describe the process as a kind of sleepwalking; he wakes, packs his bag, and finds himself firing the ignition without even realising what's happening. It's a spell-like flicker of the subconscious, beyond reproach and also beyond his control. By the time my mother has done the perfunctory checks—surgery, her parents, his sister—and phoned the police, he's already clear of the city, drifting aimlessly down the coast. He listens to talkback radio, buys cappuccinos with cash, and keeps on driving.

My father runs away with the express desire of being caught. This waking bureaucratic nightmare is his quinquennial crisis moment, the way in which men of his generation cry for help. As my mother will reason when he's tracked down for the fourth time, it could be worse. He could drink, your father. Gamble. Philander. Beat her, or you. These stoic men born of the late fifties and sixties, they push it all down until it fills them up and blackness spews out of them, a geyser of acid and molten tar.

I am fifteen the first time I am made aware of this state-wide cat-and-mouse game played between my father and his family since I was born. My mother tries vainly to convince me, as it becomes increasingly consequential, that I am not the catalyst for this waking nightmare. This behaviour is the culmination of a host of stressors, residual issues from his upbringing, she explains—but it doesn't discount the inalienable fact that the announcement of my existence is what first set him off, and has since spiralled out of control.

My father runs away, and we kids are all so self-obsessed, as children typically are, that it takes years for us to notice. His wife hides it for as long as she can, knowing that fathers are gods to their sons and daughters and that nothing breaks this cycle of worship like fallibility.

Dr Seidler is politely escorted home by police from local area commands across the Greater Sydney area, his licence plate flagged with discretion. He appears to the officers each time as he will to me: blank, unmoving and exhausted.

My father learns only one thing from his mistakes: how to spot the signs in someone else. I am never given the opportunity to run away. He keeps tabs on me far beyond the age it is appropriate, but I can't afford to move out so he and I fight viciously at the dinner table. We lacerate one another in the way that only sons cast from the same mould as their fathers can, intentionally prodding at main veins. He forgets that he ran away and will do so again, and I forget he is fragile because he so rarely shows it.

As I start to become more like him, I envy my father's luxury of running away. When I become overwhelmed without warning, my joie de vivre stomped face first into the kerb, there is nowhere I can go. Instead, I sit in the backyard among my parents' friends as Norah Jones taunts me politely from the CD stacker, and I disappear into my thoughts, trying to become nothing, just an angry soul without blood or body. The late summer sun sears the mango wedges and nectarine slices as I imagine being dead. They can't take this away from me.

There's something strange about imagining my father as a vigilante, especially when he hasn't committed any crime, but it's the only way to rationalise his details being circulated by the cops, his coordinates corroborated from concerned bystander tip-offs, and good, honest men in starched blue shirts pulling him over on the highway or ambushing him outside a roadside cafe. The idea of my father being a secret gang leader or drug smuggler honestly seems preferable to admitting he is regularly hijacked by his own mind. We never see him being walked back inside the gate, emerging from an unmarked detective vehicle with the resigned look of a kingpin staring down the barrel at 25-to-life. All we know, as we begin to grasp the severity of the out-of-control boomerang that is our dad, is that he was gone, he has returned, and that he might go again at some point. He and Mum slink to their bedroom and shut the door. We make sure the Nintendo 64 volume is high enough so we can't hear the pleading and shouting. Even as we sink into the chaos of *GoldenEye 007*, the loudest sound is the four of us collectively exhaling.

Ray begins to run away with increasing regularity. Resistant to reason, madder than medication, he returns home now without memory, having stopped off for stints in the ward where pulses rocket through his skull to neutralise his love of disappearing.

* * *

I'm the one, in a fit of jealousy-inspired ingenuity, who suggests the iPhone tracker. The phone purchased outright, on a basic plan, easily hidden near the spare tyre. Effectively that puts me in charge of setting it up and placing my own father under top-secret surveillance. Nothing about this situation strikes me as abnormal. I am simply the future looking out for the past.

With my mother fresh out of novel ways to tackle the problem, retrieval of the runaway becomes a group effort. He has taught all us boys how to drive, and this becomes his kryptonite: a squadron of his sons joining the pursuit parade while Zara is at school. Before long, he is barely making it past the CBD, his location triangulated in secret by a suburban Stasi he raised himself. Even our Aunt Linda, who manages my father's significant side hustle in public speaking, is pulled into the chase. The police, far past the limits of goodwill, are replaced by a private militia, as my siblings and I hunt down the runaway in second-hand cars with provisional licences.

In the end, he is running away with such zeal that admitting him seems like the only thing left to do.

The hospital visiting area is painted a bland, dental green that sits somewhere between spearmint and teal. It is the sort of colour that mutes thoughts before they make it to your mouth. Dad sits slumped against the wall and stares past me, unblinking. It is four days before my twenty-fifth birthday and he's due home tomorrow. I have a million questions, but none of them make it into actual sentences. As we hug goodbye for the night, somebody says 'I'm sorry,' but I can't remember who.

After just a week back home, he runs away again, never saying goodbye.

This time he doesn't come back.

He takes a trick straight out of my book, the bastard: he flees without even leaving the house.

SEVEN

To understand Linkin Park, you really need to understand Joe 'Chairman' Hahn. You might not remember or recognise Hahn, who was only 23 when the band he joined after dropping out of school became the fastest-selling act on the planet. That stands to reason; Hahn grew up watching MTV where he saw nobody who looked like him either. Call it grunge or alt-rock or nu-metal or whatever you want—it was clear to teenagers still finding themselves, like Hahn in Glendale, California, that this was a white man's game. Save for a few brown faces that managed to sneak in the side door before anyone noticed—Tony Kanal of No Doubt, Tom Morello from Rage Against the Machine—the presiding rulers of guitar music were blue-eyed, blond-haired and unquestionably 'American'.

One of the only Asian-Americans to jam a decent foot in the door was James Iha, Billy Corgan's right-hand man in Smashing Pumpkins. But Hahn's parents weren't Japanese, like Iha's or Mike Shinoda's, the latter the future bandmate he'd soon meet at Design College in Pasadena. They were Korean.

I was a diehard fan of Linkin Park for many years before I fully comprehended Joe Hahn, and a couple more before I appreciated just how vital he was to the group's operation. That's because Hahn is not somebody I would have noticed in the late nineties. There were no Asians in my class, nor my school, nor in the limited, insular suburb through which I moved—save for Sweetie, a Filipino-Bolivian who I met by accident at a house party. Given the sizeable waves of migration to Australia since at least the 1960s from Vietnam, Thailand, Cambodia, the Philippines, Korea, Japan and China, this should tell you a lot about the ways our communities chose to segregate themselves.

To me for a long time, Joe Hahn, the Chairman, also known as 'Mr Hahn', was simply the inconspicuous guy who appeared to be scratching vinyl behind a very famous, instantly recognisable white singer. He could have been anyone.

They call Hahn the Chairman because even though many fans rarely heard him speak in the early days of Linkin Park, he is one of the undeniable guiding factors to their success. Whether in footage or on stage, Hahn was often deliberately positioned in the background, spinning and scratching turntables, one of the many skills he picked up in high school. This was easier to show an audience than all the other key band activities in which his fingers were also stuck: production, sound design, samples, composition, album art and directing more than 30 music videos. He was the first ethnic Korean to win a Grammy—now he's got four. He once cast a live snake for a shoot. Several of his Linkin Park music videos, like for the songs 'Numb' and 'In the End', have been viewed more than a billion times on YouTube alone. All this from the guy you've probably forgotten about if you'd ever even heard of him at all.

The fact that the Chairman is the second most famous Asian-American *from his own band* definitely indicates how the culture has shifted since he first got behind the camera with his bandmates to shoot the clip for 'Papercut' (featuring, among other things, Mike with purple hair and Chester sporting a red mohawk with terrible tartan trousers to match). Today, Korean pop music has grown to become one of the biggest phenomena on Earth. Western music royalty like Dua Lipa and Cardi B have fallen over backwards to get BTS or Blackpink on a track, even if—especially if—they don't sing in English. But back in 1999, K-pop was mostly isolated to its country of origin, a unique form of world music that you'd only really come across if you spent time in Seoul or knew who Rain was. Linkin Park were five albums deep before

'Gangnam Style' exploded across the internet. You don't have to ask Hahn to know that's a hell of a long time.

* * *

There's a specific visual style that became commonplace in film at the turn of the millennium, where a crucial fight scene was deliberately slowed down to a juddering halt. At a particular freeze-frame, the director lingered on the moment for a second longer than was comfortable before hitting play on the action again. Some auteurs like to pin this extreme slo-mo movement to *The Matrix*, which redefined special effects for a generation of cinemagoers, particularly when it came to being able to limbo-bend away from bullets. But it was already happening across other violent free-for-alls for years, dramatics heightened by a nifty sleight of hand. When someone gets punched after one of these deliberate stopgaps—and it's almost always a punch—it feels like the character's been smacked clean out of the shot with a cricket bat, bones rattling so hard that they might collapse into dust from the impact. It's the same punch as any other—'Mah Nishtana', as we ask on Passover: 'What makes this one any different?'—but there is something enduringly fresh about this mega-whack, this winding down to ramp up, the movie equivalent of the sudden reload on a banger in the club.

As a director himself, Hahn appreciated the value of tightening in on crucial elements only to blow them back open again. His lasting contribution to Linkin Park is perhaps the most important: sound design. Much like a filmmaker, a true turntablist knows how to carry a listener along for the journey, and when to make sure they're paying attention. That glorious cinematic belter, where blood flies and teeth rattle, was purpose-built into every Linkin Park single. It's the clickety-clack train line drums that divert your ears away from the sledgehammer riff barrelling your way on 'One Step Closer'. The metallic flanger, panning in and out that rips open 'Papercut'. Vocals pinging off different channels, layer piling upon layers; this ability to slice through the density, to refocus our ears on melody and form amid a cacophony of sound, is Hahn's unsung legacy.

For many, the sight of a DJ in a rock band is an easy sign to steer clear of a genre that was very much of its time and has definitely not aged well. The Chairman was far from the only man on the wheels of steel in heavy music around the time of 9/11: there was also DJ Lethal (Limp Bizkit), DJ Starscream (Slipknot), DJ Kilmore (Incubus), DJ AM (Crazy Town) and Frank Delgado (Deftones). Many of these men were simply recruited to cram even more into an already dangerously over-stacked noise burrito, cribbing sounds from hip-hop and parsing them into white 'bro' culture. You can tell who took their job seriously; only the Chairman would be given his own track on an album to show off the versatility of his musicianship. 'Cure For the Itch', Hahn's two-and-a-half-minute rampage through the myriad styles that influenced him, appearing on Linkin Park's debut album *Hybrid Theory*, was so fundamental that it paved the way for the album to be remixed alongside some of the biggest names in rap. This was not a normal thing to happen in the year 2000.

* * *

Colin Ho burst into my life on my second day of university. He was my first friend of Chinese heritage. We were in the same tutorial and I liked him immediately; he was exactly the sort of turbo-geek I vibed with, especially when it came to music. When Colin got excited about something he was unstoppable. He fell hard and quick for new sounds and strange polyrhythms, and had no issues about not appearing cool, which naturally made him the coolest person I'd ever met. Dad liked him too, and would often sit in on our jam sessions at the old house when Colin schlepped his Fender Rhodes, amp and small army of pedals all the way from Ryde, an hour away from where we lived. Ray once told me, 'Colin's got more soul than all your other mates put together.'

Over the years, Colin became a fixture at our birthday parties and events. We started a trio and played shows together. I became a magazine editor and he wrote tech stories for me, and he guided me through my first year in London, signposting the clubs I should haunt to hear the best new UK jazz. Colin unironically loved the things he loved, which ironically made me think of Joe Hahn. I wondered if I'd been overlooking other brilliant, deep, introspective people that didn't look like the ones I grew up with.

If he hadn't been so busy tearing up my Linkin Park fan club card, Dad would have gravitated to the Chairman immediately. The upside of running a surgery that catered to hundreds of transient travellers was that Ray learned very early how to become a citizen of the world, rather than just an Australian Who Sometimes Goes On Holidays. The concept of foreigners was largely foreign to him. Everyone was on equal footing, from Colin Ho to Vito, the ancient Neapolitan who stood outside Piccolo Bar and yelled obscenities to everyone, to Nando, our camp Romagnan barber cutting classic bobs next door to the local safe injecting room.

Joe Hahn was one of the earliest members of Linkin Park. He was there the day the emerging band received demos back from one Chester Bennington, who'd sung propulsive new lead lines over songs they'd already written. At the time, the band was called Xero—now more commonly associated with one of the world's biggest accounting software platforms. It was an outfit going nowhere, and then it went somewhere. You could argue, as Jeff Blue, the A&R who eventually signed the group to Warner, has often said in interviews, that Chester was the missing piece of the puzzle. Or you could slow down the vision, spin back the sound and walk around the scene, taking in the action from a different position.

Suddenly, from every angle, there's the Chairman.

EIGHT

July has regularly been my least favourite month of the year. It's mid-winter in Sydney, a subtropical climate where the rain can be relentless and pubs don't open until mid-afternoon. Never really that cold, with the temperature rarely dipping below double digits, it's still unpleasant in a way that nobody can really put their finger on. That's why anyone with the means is usually far away at the end of July, heading at least further north, if not to the other side of the globe, which is not great news for me, as it's also when my birthday arrives.

When I turn ten, I throw a huge birthday party and nobody comes. I sit out the front of my house in a new Bart Simpson t-shirt, legs dangling off the fence, trying to look like I don't care, even though my face feels hot and it's obvious I'm embarrassed, or crying, or both. There is a tree in the front garden that wasps favour for their nests; when I was five I thwacked one such nest with a glow-in-the-dark plastic sword my parents bought me from *Disney On Ice* just to see what would happen. A swarm followed me into the house as I ran screaming for someone to save my life. I stare at that same tree, willing the wasps to come back so they can have their vengeance, poisoning me beyond salvation so that I can escape this nightmare. I don't remember who coaxes me out of this funk and past the austere living room full of quiet balloons and party hats-in-waiting to go and order pizza, but it likely isn't my father. Well accustomed to being abandoned, but uncomfortable doing the comforting, he is out the back mowing the lawn, silently fuming. In the coming days he will track down my friends' parents and demand answers. It isn't fair. He just won't stand for it. He tempers his fury by methodically cutting the grass in concentric squares, the old two-stroke belching fumes up onto the wooden verandah.

Meanwhile, in the front seat of the trusty green family Tarago on the way to Papa's Pizza, I am formulating a different plan. There will never be a July like this again. From now on I will throw the biggest and best parties and everyone will talk about them at school. I will be surrounded by hordes of people, buzzing wasps that do not sting; they will love and admire me. This story will disappear because there will be no more sad times to compare it to. Every July will be a Good July.

Nestled into the passenger seat, I close my eyes against the late-afternoon sun and dream of a future in which I am obscenely popular, my parties no longer a cause for parental concern but now the stuff of legend.

* * *

Fifteen years on, in the midst of one such legendary event, I take a double dose of MDMA on a whim and don't come down for two days.

I've rolled into a terrace house, right around the corner from the Surry Hills pub that I'd booked out where my friends took over so many tables they had to head to the basement for more chairs. Splitting the bill had been a nightmare, but the intense actuarial precision required had filled me with joy. It's a Friday night, and all these people had been arguing over who ate parmigiana and how many beers they'd each drunk, and they were all present because of me.

(I never truly grow out of this obsession with optimising my birthday, even after relocating to London for a few years, where by rights I should have far fewer friends. By the time my thirty-first birthday rolls around, my English girlfriend, Keren, acutely aware of the unnecessary weight I attribute to dud July events, sets about organising a proper party at a local pub. I secretly invite everyone she knows, because I still don't do birthdays by half, and besides, I'm planning on proposing to her 24 hours prior with a ring that's been hiding in my Adidas trackie bottoms for the last week.)

At the house party afterwards I immediately drink a heavily spiked vodka soda without realising that I'll soon be sunk into a couch listening to the first Kings of Leon album on repeat with my on-again off-again university lover, trying valiantly to summon an erection but mostly unable to do anything except stare unblinking at the ceiling in an MDMA vortex and pray that I'm not going to die.

At a celebratory lunch with my parents the following afternoon in Potts Point, Dad and I are both zombies, but for entirely different reasons. He's just emerged from a last-ditch emergency round of ECT, which has mangled his brain like the inside of the old lawnmower. He is trying to feel again, but the journey through his neurons is slow. Mine are similarly frazzled, and the two of us say nothing as we sit in a booth with Mum, me trying to weigh up, as I gaze blithely into my lamb entrecôte, if this is indeed a Good July.

Dad's mood vexes me, and the comedown I can't admit to isn't helping. It seems like he's stopped trying, even though he's always on my back about looking after my own mental health. Mum is exhausted, which only makes matters worse; this lunch is a stick of dynamite begging for a match. I can't eat a thing, he's not hungry either, so Mum spends $180 for the three of us to silently push food around our plates.

As I say goodbye, frustrated, Dad tries to say something loving and encouraging, but he can't quite get it out. I roll my eyes and get into my car, driving home distractedly to sit in my apartment alone on my birthday, chain-smoking cigarettes and chugging orange juice, having feelings not entirely dissimilar from when I was ten years old.

That evening Dad phones, likely at the behest of his wife, to offer an olive branch to his firstborn. I screen the call and go back to sleep. Whatever he says goes to a mailbox connected to nothing, another misfiring synapse.

When he dies a few days later, I can't stop thinking about what words he might have left. I also can't bear to find out. I wipe my voicemail inbox just to be sure.

NINE

Attunga, an Aboriginal word for 'high place', is the name of a street you would never know about if you did not grow up here. Maybe your city or town is better laid out, or entirely flat, or there are no streets to speak of. It's set deep into the hills of Woollahra, so stupendously vertical that it is practically mythical, like something written by the Ancient Greeks, an impossible shrug in the face of inevitable questions around basic physics, an incline that sneers at joggers, makes mince-meat of pedestrians, turns four-wheel drives into flimsy toys. Its sudden advance seems to wallop you in the face, as scary to climb up as it is to roll down, basically a fucking death trap that would be more at home as a Luna Park attraction than a suburban thoroughfare.

As it so happens, the foot of Attunga Street meets the base of an equally ludicrous, snaking passage masquerading as a road. And it is at this particular intersection, where simply arriving with your vehicle unscathed means good fortune has momentarily smiled upon you, that the number 630 bus bringing my sister back from school has one of its last stops before it's too late.

Attunga, death mountain that it is, has become the unfortunate site of an urgent intervention. If Zara stays on course just a few minutes longer, if she gets off the bus and walks home, she will see what I have only just driven away from: the ambulances and cop cars, the crime scene tape, the stretcher being unloaded—an NCIS-level scene taking over the street in which she has grown up and the only house she can really remember. She will probably know even before she reaches Attunga; Zara is precociously sharp for a sixteen-year-old, having lived with the Knowledge and Shame longest of all of us—being the youngest turning out to be more of a burden than a blessing. She grew up cognisant and careful as a child, has been terrified as a teenager, and is already having trouble sleeping. She's a kid on the cusp of becoming an adult in the golden age of mental health awareness, but that age is still a few years off and it's not going to help her today, en route to Attunga, where I'm idling in my car, feeling so sick that I might throw up or shit myself or maybe even both at the same time, gazing through the windscreen at that heart attack hill and wondering exactly what tone I'm supposed to take when telling my beloved baby sister, my absolute favourite person on this planet, that her father, who is her absolute favourite person on this planet, is dead in our house, dead because he decided, just as Zara fretted was going to happen but nobody took her seriously enough.

Everything happening at such warp speed since Mum first called me at the office means that I'm still jacked up on adrenalin, rushing into action instead of actually sitting with the fucking magnitude of what has just occurred. I know that the second Zara opens the car door, the minute she sees my face, it's curtains.

It's a rudely warm day for the middle of July but I'm shivering uncontrollably as I watch buses that belong to other schools inch their way down the sharp curves of the hill. I know the 630. I rode that thing for five years, fighting with the popular kids to get their attention while passing on misfortune to those even further down the food chain than myself. A carriage full of screaming private-school kids of both sexes flirting so wildly it sounds like fighting. It's never more than ten minutes late, reeking of lunchtime sweat, damp swimming costumes, dirty socks, firm-hold hair gel, Rexona, Impulse, Lip Smackers, Hubba Bubba and Juicy Fruit. Air never smells as fresh as when you step off the 630.

Zara is at that fundamentally fucked-up age where it is impossible to lie to her—too old to have the wool pulled over her eyes and too young not to be reduced to rubble by the news I'm carrying. I belch out of nervousness, trying to clear my chest passages that are closing up in anxiety, searching for cigarettes I don't have, cursing my brothers for being overseas and leaving me to do this alone, before realising with sickening certainty that it's going to be my job to tell them too. I check the rear-view mirror again, and like clockwork the 630 rolls into view. Kids tumble out of both doors like a rising tide until finally, I spot her.

Zara opens the passenger door, shoves in her school bag and nestles into the seat. She looks at me expectantly—it's not every day she gets chauffeur service. I wait for her to fill the silence, but she doesn't say anything. A spasming gut indicates that I've grossly misread the situation; Zara has no idea what is going on. And that's precisely when it all goes out the window at the bottom of Attunga, cortisol flooding my brain so quickly I can't even remember what it is that I eventually ended up getting out of my mouth. The only enduring memory I have is of sound: something between moaning and screaming, filling the car from every angle, clawing up the sides, surging and sloshing below the seats, pushing so hard against the metal that it begins to buckle, twisting and gnarling under the pressure and when I come to, it is all blasting from Zara, head slammed forward against the dash like we've somehow had a catastrophic accident while still being parked, howling without words, such long vowels, her voice always deeper and hoarser than her peers, almost guttural. I am holding it together, and then I am not, the facade splintering and sonic waves throbbing through the car; spit, snot, saliva, saline, all of it whirling like a cyclone, until finally, it breaks free and storms up Attunga, levelling the once-formidable ascent to ash.

Our grief, ultimately, is awkward. It is rapid sweat, unusual, dank smell, red eyes, stammering, open-ended sentences, uncontrollable howling. The sensation not unlike casually putting one's hand on an electric stove you were not aware was burning: clumsy and all-consuming. There is no elegant way out of it, even as the hurricane pouring from Zara's chest slowly starts to weaken. Now, in the place of a clean continuum, is a litter of debris, a clearly defined Before and After. Realising this, as we both do in real time, makes for confronting viewing. All I want are the words to move us out of this lingering take. We are the last people to relish this sort of awkwardness. It does not agree with our temperaments. Memories begin to shatter and collapse. This one moment is stretching on for an eternity.

It is the kind of moment you either remember forever or spend forever trying to repress. Either way, you are unlucky.

I often wonder what it would have been like to have been a passer-by on Attunga that afternoon, perhaps walking the dog or on the way to get coffee. How loud it had to be before a car is nothing but a prop and all you can see is two siblings cracking apart as dusk falls on the worst day of their lives. Maybe you're concerned, and you hover nearby, just to make sure something untoward isn't happening where you might need to step in or call the police. Or maybe you just keep on walking uphill, knowing that without momentum Attunga will surely flatten you, content to simply take home the story of the children you saw sitting in a car today, seatbelts on, going nowhere and absolutely crying their eyes out.

Zara is the last of us to go to the same school, which now has such a large intake of new students that each year group has ballooned well beyond 120 children. If you count the primary kids on the same campus, that's in excess of 1000 hyperactive Jewish kids trying to get home; far too many to fit onto the one bus per route. As per, the second 630 has just arrived. Kids amble out, a few of them who Zara knows. This is mission critical; we can't stay here any longer. It's like we've been caught defiling something sacred. We don't want anyone we recognise laying eyes on us.

I jolt the ancient engine into gear and we start moving. Attunga soon looms in the rear-view, quietly promising to hold on to our secrets. There will be more to come, but for the moment, it's silent inside the car.

We're in a poignant movie scene we absolutely don't want to be in. None of the dialogue seems to fit anymore. The director wisely changes shot, pulling out of the interior and zooming out on the Astra as it winds its way through the suburban streets on its way back to the hastily police-taped family home. And there's a really perfect song playing throughout. The music supervisor didn't know if they could get clearance, but as soon as she showed the singer-songwriter's team a rough cut of the scene they got the green light. It's called 'Siren Song', a haunting, British noir ballad by Bat for Lashes. The arrangement is soaked in pathos, intuiting everything the characters can't say. It moves gracefully between solo legato piano and a sudden, swelling orchestral chorus, one that effortlessly reaches through the skin and pummels the heart to pieces.

As the car rounds the final bend onto our street, Zara and I still can't speak, staring intently out the window at nothing. There are lyrics, and they're relevant, but the maelstrom of soprano and strings is far more important. It's what everyone behind the camera is banking on. In the final few weeks it will not be unusual to see seasoned editors breaking down behind the monitors in the darkened post-production suite.

That's the thing about tragedy: it's much more poetic when it happens to someone else.

TEN

When it becomes blindingly obvious that I am never going to take to any sport, group or otherwise, Dad drags me to the gym. By the first year of high school I've made it abundantly clear that I'm not even remotely interested in conventional fitness. I'm plainly no good at anything P.E. related. I can't shoot hoops. I kick own goals. Even when I try to game the system by racing the special needs kids at the athletics carnival, I still come dead last. Meanwhile, David is blossoming into a minor Olympian, tearing up the ranks to reach State for both swimming and running. At only eleven years old he is already taller and broader than me. Soon Zac will join him. Despite having two average-sized parents, both my younger brothers will eventually end up well over six feet before they finish high school. In the meantime, Mum books me in with a paediatrician who gently suggests a series of hormone shots to help kickstart my adolescence. Though I've only just had a bar mitzvah, it seems nobody is convinced I have the right stuff to become a man.

We don't have cable at our house, so the gym's only saving grace is continuous access to MTV. The men I truly look up to have ripped bodies by virtue of jumping around on stage, shredding solos on their knees or thrashing the bejesus out of a drum kit each night. Two decades after the excesses of glam, there is still an astounding level of shirtlessness in rock and roll. My walls are adorned in full-length posters of Anthony Kiedis and Brandon Boyd, beautiful, long-haired frontmen with sinewy bodies chiselled from mountains. They out-muscle Ray, who I once thought was the strongest man on the planet but to my teenage eyes seems more like a compact vehicle covered in shag carpeting. Even Chester Bennington, a twig by eighties frontman standards, looks jacked in photographs. I do not want to end up like my dad. I want to be feared and desired in equal measure, just like them.

'The gym is *great*,' Dad says in a voice that tells me he's been reading that popular self-help book called *Raising Boys* again. 'You move at your own pace and can go whenever you want. It's fantastic for the body and the mind.' He is standing in my room, observing the shrine to alternative rock that is slowly taking over all available real estate. Dave Navarro winks, wearing leather pants, eyeliner and a perfect sixpack. Meticulously cut out and fastened with Blu Tack, Josh Homme's inked biceps ripple out of his cut-off tee. You can almost feel the testosterone and distortion seeping from the walls. I roll my eyes because this is what is clearly required of me and swivel back to my computer.

Taking my teenage drollness for approval, Dad signs me up for the local gym near his surgery in what is undeniably one of the gay capitals of Sydney. Bayswater Gym is populated exclusively by hairless, bulging men on cruising missions. They regard my twig arms with indifference.

'Don't try and lift something heavier than you can manage,' Dad warns. 'It's a slow process, not a race.' He is convinced that excessive weight use stunts growth, and I am pipsqueak enough already. But I cannot stop staring at my fellow gym members. The narrow vision of ultimate manhood I've been pursuing is suddenly all out of whack. They have expertly groomed facial hair, sick sneakers and perfect physiques. They kiss one another hello and are always making plans. It's a combination of strength and softness I didn't know was possible, and it rattles me. 'If you don't stop staring like that, one of these boys might take you home,' Dad jokes. He guides me through rows, push-ups and shoulder presses. He tells me not to forget sit-ups, which I do. Everything hurts. At night I flex in front of the mirror. My triceps are sad whoopee cushions. I think about the boys at Bayswater. Dad has told me not to be disillusioned, but I can't help it. This will never work.

Eventually I get that long overdue growth spurt and my parents move on to other projects, but the gym remains a fixture for me. Lord knows why I decide to stick with it. I've given up everything else physical with zero qualms, even convincing our teachers that tenpin bowling and chess are legitimate sports so that my last few years of school can be mercifully perspiration-free.

I move to a makeshift club with ancient 20kg plates and rusting, sweat-encrusted machines, and I get pretty good at it. The local rugby boys let me play Linkin Park and Queens of the Stone Age on the battered stereo when they're done with their mix CDs. They never talk to me on the street, but here they spot me as I pump out reps. They think I want to join the try-outs, but I just want to look nothing at all like my father.

* * *

I'm in my late twenties and it's no longer acceptable to play bruising, belting rock music at parties anymore. In the great culture war of my youth I've backed the wrong side. Hip-hop has become the dominant genre—actually, more like the overarching aesthetic—of my era. Innovative, radical and chimerical, it spins off in a million different directions, a limitless spider web of influences, samples, sounds and voices. Rock, meanwhile, pales in significance, both on the Top 40 and in contemporary culture. It remains vital only in the matt pages of *Rolling Stone* and the newsprint grubbiness of *NME*, with dwindling readerships that will soon write them both out of newsstands altogether.

Punk struggles along, as it always has, scrappy and resilient. Prog returns every two years for a new class of stoners that somehow missed both the sixties, seventies and early nineties. But the biggest acts in the world? They're rappers. Kanye West and Kendrick Lamar, Skepta and Stormzy, Travis Scott and A$AP Rocky. Their names are glam glitter; KISS without makeup. It's the culture that swallows the globe; album covers dreamed up by cult Japanese artists, expensive videos directed by French mavericks, clothing capsule collaborations with Adidas, beats hijacked from Jamaica, Nigeria and Brazil. Hip-hop, ever evolving, is unstoppable.

Ground zero for this sea change is the gym. They're all part of chain brands now, even my old club, emblazoned with loud logos in primary colours and even louder music blasting out of screens that seem to plaster every spare corner. The treadmill has a TV. The cross-trainer has a TV. There are TVs in the changerooms. All of them play an almost constant rotation of top tier hip-hop, which has even started seeping into electronic music, perfecting the sort of relentless, optimised beats with which Silverchair and Soundgarden just cannot compete. This is the shiny new sound of the future. The weights are cleaned daily; plates are always replaced.

Each available surface always appears freshly wiped down. Along with the banter, camaraderie and casual misogyny, the grit of the gym has gone. It is the next golden era of rap and it sounds as expensive as it looks. Suddenly my crappy old t-shirts don't cut it as training gear anymore. The rugby boys are bankers and real estate agents now. They wear $260 box-fresh trainers and slick trackies. Everyone constantly drinks creatine shakes.

It feels like I am thirteen again.

Rockstars themselves will tell you they don't make much of a dent on the conversation anymore. This new guard knows no rules. They splash my generation's deities across re-upped Marc Jacobs tees, pilfering the magazine spreads of the bygone era still clinging to my childhood bedroom wall for sartorial inspiration. The noughties usher in rappers with small prefixes and huge personas. Lil Uzi Vert, the Marilyn Manson acolyte. Lil Peep, the codeine-dependent Linkin Park tragic. Lil Wayne kickflipping his skateboard into a duet with Blink-182.

Even the lyrics pay homage. On the 'XO Tour Llif3'—the high watermark of emo's crossover into hip-hop—Lil Uzi Vert sighs 'Push me to the edge / All my friends are dead' through a vocoder. It's only a few power chords shy of My Chemical Romance. They play it at my gym every fifteen minutes.

* * *

I have preserved two safe places for my treasured collection of Music To Slit Your Wrists By. The first is my fourteen-year-old Astra—stuck at the same difficult age I was when I first got a gym membership—that only plays CDs. Fittingly, the car is infested with spiders and smells like death.

The other more shameful outlet is a private playlist, downloaded onto every device I own for posterity, because even though my generation ushered this technology into being, we're still slightly unnerved by files this weightless. Saving songs as hard megabytes onto hard drives now has its own significance. It says 'I am willing to crash my phone for this album. I am willing for this to be one of the only things I can listen to when I have no available data in a foreign country.' It's an invisible, buffer-free commitment.

On this playlist festers close to two decades' worth of combined noise, the kind that once alienated my parents, and will presumably, in some not-too-distant future, do the same to my kids. It runs the gamut from Rage Against the Machine to Offspring, Deftones to Refused. Even the softest cuts on this collection don't stay that way for long. It is white hot Semtex.

This playlist is called 'Gym'.

This is what has become of my beloved angry anthems, relegated to high-intensity F45 classes, synced to NRL coverage. It appears that sites of mega-octane fitness are the only places these songs remain contextually appropriate, and even then, only through noise-cancelling headphones. In the Gym of Tomorrow there is music all around, but nobody is actually listening to it. We are all sealed off in our own private Idahos and mine is blisteringly loud. Nobody talks to anyone, nor offers to watch over them as they handle heavy dumbbells.

* * *

It's between bench press sets in 2017 in this slick utopia of personal betterment that I flick open Twitter and discover Chester Bennington has died. It is doubly auspicious, commenters soon note, as it is also Chris Cornell's birthday. Both men have taken their own lives only months apart from one another. Bennington sang at Cornell's funeral. He was the godfather to Cornell's son. This is some Illuminati-level stuff.

Today is also my birthday.

I take my headphones off. Post Malone is warbling vaguely melodic hip-hop through the armada of screens. He is holding a guitar. I know he can play it, but it still looks like a prop.

I sit motionless. From my sweat-lined cans my gym playlist blares on.

Staring at the blank tweet box, knowing I have to write something, anything, I realise I've been listening to Linkin Park for half my natural life. It's moved from public to private, this little ember of my old self that refuses to die out even after all the scrawled black Converse with odd laces, ripped jeans with anarchist patches and studded bracelets have long since been relegated to the tip. This is the music I heard when I was fighting to enter puberty, and it was new and exciting, and now its central figure is dead.

I'm so sorry, Chester, I type quickly. *Thank you for the rawness and honesty you brought to a particularly disaffected generation.*

From the screen next to my weight station, DJ Khaled yells his own name. I walk back around the bench, racking up another 10kg on each side. Over the driving beat, I hear Dad's voice starting to tell me off. 'You don't have to prove anything,' he says, translucent behind the weight rack. 'This isn't a contest.' But he's long since lost the right to tell me what to do. All the big, strong men I looked up to in my life are disappearing.

Chester's demise is trending. Suicide by hanging. He was also a father. This cannot be happening again. I'm not sure I can handle it.

Dad hangs back silently behind the weight rack, aware he's overstepped the line. My newsfeed is now exploding with grief:

This album was all time. Still is. So sad.

It's fucked up that this can happen to anyone, let alone some dude who was in a huge band and had six kids etc. World needs some work.

Such emotion in all his lyrics, he was a true gift to all his fans.

His music really spoke to me. It was a big part of my youth.

This bench press bar is now definitely too heavy, but I don't ask anyone to spot me as I scroll all the way to the top of 'Gym', where Linkin Park's 'Papercut' remains the very first song on the list after all these years.

I know I'm going to have to make a choice. You physically can't cry and bench 90kg at the same time. Between my Left and Right channels, nobody else can change the station. The juggernaut riff swells into being. Mike Shinoda's opening lines echo forebodingly:

Why does it feel like night today?
Something in here's not right today.

Eyes closed.

Block it out.

Inhale.

Exhale.

Push.

I want this to hurt.

ELEVEN

From: Jonathan Seidler
To: Aryeh Tal
18 July 2019.

Dear Aryeh,

Thank you so much for taking the time to see me today, and I'm overjoyed that you approve of the question I'll be asking your incredible daughter on Friday.

However, as I sit on the train back to London, it occurs to me that I haven't been entirely straight with you—and that this isn't how I want to start a new chapter of my life.

When we had lunch, you mentioned 'skeletons in closets'. I believe you were making sure I had nothing to hide, which is obviously a hangover from Keren's previous relationship. I don't blame you for asking the question.

She's very important to you and you do not want to see her hurt.

With that in mind, I want to tell you about my skeleton. Keren is aware of this and may have discussed it with you, but it's also entirely possible that she hasn't. I believe—as do my family—that too many lives are ruined by a lack of transparency and honesty between families. As you are soon going to be my family, I think it should only be fair that you are aware of what I bring to this partnership.

So. I have bipolar disorder. Specifically, I have bipolar II disorder, which is the less severe version. That being said, it is an illness and it is real. It's also hereditary.

I bring this up with you for two reasons. Firstly, my father had depression, and nobody in his family ever told my mother before they got married. She had to find out the hard way, and it's to her credit that she managed to raise a huge family and have a happy marriage until my father passed away. You may also be aware that my father died by suicide, or perhaps you are not. These things are related, but thankfully unique to his condition, which was different from my own.

The biggest issue of my father's generation is that men did not talk about their feelings. I'm exceptionally lucky that my lot has learned from their mistakes. But that means telling you that I am not always perfect. There are days when I am not well. Sometimes I get depressed, and occasionally it's very bad. Sometimes I am up, sometimes I am down. There are lots of people like me out there. You probably know a few among your friends in Israel. We are larger than life people and we love life. It can get too much for us on occasion, but luckily for me I have many outlets to talk about it, including Keren.

I've been on stable medication for a decade and have not had any serious episodes lately. I've had regular psychological check-ins since my early 20s. But that's not the point.

A skeleton is still a skeleton and this is mine. I want to give you the full knowledge that nobody gave my parents (or my parents' parents), because love without complete honesty is a promise not worth the paper it's written on. I apologise for not telling you in person, but I'm here to talk about it any time you like.

I want you to know that I have been happier in the past year than I have since I was a teenager. That I feel safe and secure and happy with Keren, and that she is, as you said, the most loyal and wonderful person I could have wished for. I think the two of us together are unstoppable and that we can help each other through anything. I have few doubts that we will be together for as long as we are alive. We are a stupendously great match.

Finally, it's also been fantastic getting to know you better, because the more time I spend with you the more you remind me of my father. Like you, he was a wonderfully warm man with lots of friends and an incredible ear for music. I have missed him so much during this process, but with you I feel significantly less alone.

I look forward to celebrating next week as your official son-in-law,

Yours,
Jonathan.

TWELVE

In retrospect, I don't think there's any cosmic significance to 'Lean on Me', the incredibly popular ballad by one of history's most brilliant songwriters. The song's very construction is charming to anyone with even a passing interest in music, chords rising and falling in almost perfect symmetry. It's devilishly simple, as many of the most enduring songs are, but even at an amateur level its performance produces a certain theatrical flair. I know this because by the time I am a teenager I have heard my dad play and sing this song about a thousand times.

Still, it is slightly strange that of the 150-odd numbers in the *Singalong Standards* book Dad buys in 1998 at a garage sale for $3, the Bill Withers number is the one that sticks. 'Summertime' could have stood in just as easily. 'The Girl From Ipanema'. 'Hey Jude'. Anything that doesn't cold-open with 'Sometimes in our lives / we all have pain / we all have sorrow.'

The piano has trailed us from house to house. It's a Yamaha upright in honey-brown maple, and Dad always insists on it having pride of place even though nobody knows how to play it properly. From a young age we learn the concept of myth-making—that if you surround yourself with the key accoutrements of any artistic pursuit, you will eventually convince yourself and everyone around you that it's one in which you are proficient.

Dad is not strictly a musician, but clearly has the ear. He can sing in tune, harmonise, bash out swing rhythms. Someone must have taught him the building blocks at some point in his life because he can read sheet music and plough his way through a jazz standard after only five minutes in front of the score. He knows his circle of fifths, understands blues construction and is acquainted with the dark art of improvisation. This despite his frankfurter fingers, stocky little fat things that bulge beneath his wedding band and can barely manage to splay out for a regular arpeggio. The music is in him.

We all take turns at piano lessons but it never really sticks. The music gene instead resolves itself in louder, more Seidler-appropriate instruments. Two drummers and a sax player later, our house is hosting rehearsals for makeshift punk and funk bands every other weekend. It is an unceasing din, and in the few moments of quiet, one of us always sits down to tinkle at the piano just because it's there.

(An incomplete list of the songs I can still play from memory on the piano: 'Für Elise', 'Chopsticks', 'Cruella De Ville' from *101 Dalmatians*, the *Mission Impossible* theme.)

In a dramatic reconfiguring of the downstairs floor plan, it is decided that the piano no longer belongs in the multi-purpose TV room where it resembles a piece of weird, mismatched furniture more than an instrument, but rather at the base of the house's central staircase. This proves to be a terrible decision for a number of reasons, prime among them being that having it casually hanging out in such an open space means everyone feels compelled to bash its keys all the time.

* * *

I am too young to realise that Dad is drawn to 'Lean on Me' because it is a piece of music that lyrically functions as a mask. No matter how dark and hopeless my father feels, the song acts as a corrective. The more angst you push through the melody, the better it sounds. Cleverly, it allows the performer to offer help when they are in fact asking for it. When it comes to artistic catharsis, it's perhaps the polar opposite of a band like Linkin Park, who by their very nature invite the listener to revel in and extract power from sadness. 'Lean on Me' is a tree; sucking in poison, replacing it with oxygen.

It will be years before I appreciate all the other fantastic songs Withers wrote—and there are a lot of them: 'Use Me', 'Ain't No Sunshine', 'Who Is He (and What Is He to You)?', 'Grandma's Hands', 'Lovely Day'. But I remain haunted and transfixed by Withers' unmistakeable timbre in 'Lean on Me'. Rumour has it that he wrote this song on a dinky toy piano when he was close to being homeless. You can hear that edge in his voice. It is so honest it slices right through. It is what they mean when they call someone a 'soul singer'; not necessarily devout in the traditional sense, but able to channel vast swathes of human experience simply by holding a note or attacking a phrase in a certain way.

The song is a naked grasp for hope.

* * *

We three sons are singing 'Lean on Me' and there are security guards posted outside the front of the house. Because we are Jewish, because Israel is between two Intifadas and because this is an unusually large gathering you'd be forgiven for thinking this is a safety precaution. And, in a way, you'd be right on the money. We do have the threat of a security breach. It's just that the bad actor is already inside. The two guards with one neck between them have been employed with strict instructions to keep Dad in.

It's David's bar mitzvah, and Mum has gone to extra-ordinary lengths to transform our architecturally confused

home into a bespoke entertainment venue. Somewhat ingeni-
ously, she's extended a marquee from the front balcony across
the garden, doubling the floor plan of the house. All the
furniture has been removed, piled high in bedrooms which
have become obstacle courses, and shoved into spare nooks.
Trestles are hauled in, a riser is set up for the band, and
crates of hired glassware, crockery and cutlery appear hourly.
The house is a fucking war zone, which would be stressful
for most husbands but for Dad it's about three steps over
the ledge. Aside from bemoaning the cost of this enterprise
he doesn't say much. His expression is permanently fixed in
that Steve Martin in *Father of the Bride* mash-up of grin and
grimace—the sign of a man palpably battling a breakdown
while trying to be supportive.

It so happens that David's rite of passage has collided
with our awareness of Dad's inability to integrate high-stress,
complicated life events. It had been recently decided that we
boys were all now old enough to be let in on the secret that our
father can occasionally be a menace, entirely lacking in mental
fortitude or self-control. This is a point Mum clearly does not
want to expand on with us, exasperated and in the middle
of marshalling industrial quantities of smoked salmon into
borrowed eskies. But the presence of our own rented Mossad
has made that impossible—we clearly know something's up.
We are not rich or interesting enough to justify their existence,

hovering outside the gate in their ill-fitting suits and unsubtle earpieces that dangle like old telephone cords.

We have not realised that Dad hasn't spent the last few nights at home. Present when required, he is in the midst of a serious unravelling, and given the choice to go back to hospital or take some time out, he's opted to hole up at our grandmother's house so as not to make a scene. He's chosen Oma, his mother-in-law, over the mother he grew up with. This says something, but who knows what. Each night he lies fitfully in the single bedroom Mum grew up in, with its creaking Hungarian furniture, 1960s light fixtures and giant mirror with Elvis decal, silently chastising himself for letting it get this bad. That the three of us boys know things are wrong, but not exactly how wrong, is by design. Across the family there is an implicit understanding that the less us teenagers know, the better. For his part, Dad conjures up the requisite amount of sparkle to almost have us believe that everyone's worrying about nothing. A bar mitzvah is a big event. The community is watching.

The benefit of having three sons in brief succession is not just being able to dress them in identical OshKosh B'Gosh denim dungarees when they are little, but also having them perform party tricks for guests as they grow. So it is that we end up warbling 'Lean on Me', this song our father introduced to us, my voice at fifteen still pushing back against puberty, a trio of castrati with saucer eyes and hairy upper lips. We harmonise by singing the exact same note in the same octave—Dad watching on, entirely dissociated—to an audience of fawning friends and family that numbers close to a hundred. Nobody has prepared us for this: a real-time lesson in irony, assuming the persona of strong, soulful men when we are, all of us, disintegrating. We sing with one eye on the lyric sheet, the other on the outside stairs. For a boisterous man, our father can vanish silently. He went on the lam only a few days ago. The keyboard plonks, the bongos slap. We sing, and we watch our guests delight at this celebration of confusion.

For a horrible moment, Dad disappears from view. We all notice at the same time, but we are rendered powerless by the performance we are bang in the middle of. There are at least two verses left before we're allowed to escape; telepathically we discuss if that will be enough time to stop a sick man on autopilot. Maybe he's slipped over the fence and through the neighbour's yard, eluding the guards. Or ducked out the back, past the madhouse of the kitchen where dessert is being prepared.

But no, he's nowhere out there because he's here, stepping up to the microphone next to his sons, unable to resist the chance to lay out his pain in plain view and see if anyone notices. That diminutive flight risk of a man has been pushed aside by Our Father, and lo, he's singing full throttle, back to claim himself from himself, even if only for these precious few minutes. The guests are delighted. They clap enthusiastically and out of time, marvelling at what a wonderful harmonious family this is as Dad launches into the final verse.

The goateed keyboardist plonks dutifully behind us. Event bands are well-accustomed to this sort of interference; he doesn't drop a note. And if you close your eyes and shut out all the forks scraping plates and the humming of gossip and the refilling of glasses, if you deflate all the pomp and ceremony and wriggle us out of these uncomfortable shirts that button up too close to our Adam's apples, it's just Dad and us, at the piano by the stairs, singing because we feel like it. The melody flows spontaneously, our voices an octave higher than Ray's, the past and the present combining on a lazy Sunday afternoon, free of the future knowledge of what this song means, what it will mean.

It's a memory so tactile you could reach out and feel the edges. David sits on the stool next to Zac, who is on my lap. Their baby fingers sound out the chords slowly, Dad watching, guiding them to the right notes. 'The root is what you hear in the bass,' he says. 'Your left hand. So that's a C.' We move over and watch as he performs the progression without even pausing to think about it. Zac's five-year-old eyes open wide. Our dad is absolutely incredible.

'If there is a load / you have to bear / that you can't ca-rry . . .'

Everyone assumes we are tearing up because it is a simcha.

THIRTEEN

To understand Linkin Park, you really need to try to understand Limp Bizkit. It's difficult, I know. Just ask my dad, who spent most of his early fifties trying to ignore both bands blasting out of multiple rooms of our house. These two ear-crushing collectives of angry American men are so close in the rock alphabet that if you found yourself flipping through the racks at HMV, Tower Records or Sanity Music during the tail end of the CD era, it wouldn't be surprising to find their records mixed in with one another. Certainly most parents hated them equally.

There are still far too many people out there who think Limp Bizkit and Linkin Park are the same band. This is the unfortunate reality of having phonetically similar names, album covers that crib from street art, and clear overlaps in the overuse of multi-channel guitar. Both prominently feature rappers who aren't Black spitting turbo-charged bars over riffs so slickly produced and frankly fucking cavernous that they make their sonic forefathers House of Pain and Faith No More sound like scrappy punk bands. Every generation gets the moral panic it deserves—my mother and Oma once had a huge fight over Elvis—but really, there can't have been anything quite as terrifying as trying to control a teenager in a decade that minted Trent Reznor, Brian 'Marilyn Manson' Warner, Jonathan Davis, Corey Taylor, Chester Bennington and William Frederick 'Fred' Durst.

A classic aphorism was thrown around a lot in my early career when I was stuck on shit creative briefs in advertising agencies: a rising tide lifts all boats. Allegedly coined by JFK, it relates to the idea that if an economy is performing well then everyone participating in it will, too. It's neat, quotable and works in almost every setting, unless the fleet you're talking about has been christened 'nu-metal' and the tide is Fred Durst. Limp Bizkit managed a feat few other bands at the peak of their powers will match: tanking their entire genre while somehow still managing to outsell most of their fellow artists. Definitely not the only group of their oeuvre of questionable quality, Durst & Co. had the most outsized impact; a roaring bin fire that somehow kept racking up sales across the globe. The writing should have been on the wall in 1994 when they were running around Hollywood desecrating George Michael's 'Faith', but by the time Middle

America—and by extension, much of Australia, including concerned Jewish fathers in Eastern Sydney—realised what they were up to, they were already an unstoppable phenomenon.

Words cannot accurately describe how much I adored Limp Bizkit, an absolutely awful band, when I was thirteen. I was far from the only one; hormonal, acne-scarred kids in Volcom t-shirts the world over boosted the band's terribly titled *Chocolate Starfish and the Hot Dog Flavored Water* to one million sales in a single week upon debut. It remains one of the few records in contemporary music history to achieve these crazy numbers while simultaneously being awarded multiple gongs for 'Worst Album of the Year'. But even a teenager with a loose grip on anything related to skill could tell you that the talent in the group—if you could call it that—wasn't situated at the front. The band featured a fluid guitarist who played strange seven-strings and often appeared in full body paint, a jazz-trained bassist, and a drummer well-versed in polyrhythm, all of whom combined for the full-frontal groove on 'Re-Arranged' and those crisp ride cymbal ad-libs sparring with reverb-laden lead lines across 'Take A Look Around'. The most enduring Limp Bizkit moments would turn out to be where Durst wasn't. I say this with the benefit of hindsight, of course. In 2000, all I cared about was blasting Bizkit's 'My Generation' from my Logitech speakers like The Who never happened, headbanging around my bedroom while screaming

'We don't—don't give a fuck and / we won't ever give a fuck un / til you—you give a fuck about me, and my generation.'

I mean, come on. What's not to love?

Arguably the apotheosis of awful when it comes to all things Limp Bizkit is 'Hot Dog', a song I unfortunately know far too well because it is seared into my cerebrum – alongside the third verse of 'Baby Got Back' and the video for Blink 182's 'What's My Age Again?' 'Hot Dog' is a song so terrible that it actively brags about the number of times it deploys the word 'fuck' and wears it as a badge of honour. It's the kind of song we used to request at bar mitzvahs, jacked up on Fanta and testosterone, jumping around and swearing with our baggy jeans and frosted tips, to terrorise our parents. The song revels in anger, in the entitlement of being a young, sexually supercharged man and not getting what you feel is owed to you. 'Hot Dog' is one of the many reasons nu-metal got such a bad rap—because it truly was the absolute worst rap. In the shock and awe stakes, it sat in diametric opposition to Eminem's searing debut *The Slim Shady LP*, which, while also vile, was definitely not dumb. From the safe vantage point of adulthood, one gets the impression that Fred Durst—whose schtick pre-empted the roiled-up, MAGA hat–wearing frat boy by nearly twenty years and whose recklessness presided over multiple out-of-control mosh pits in which young fans were critically injured or died—really only got into music to get laid and watch shit get destroyed.

Swearing is awesome when you're thirteen, especially when you combine it with drop-D guitars, a ton of distortion and absolutely no semblance of melody. But the work doesn't hold up that well, especially in Durst's case. He was an of-the-moment frontman who couldn't really sing, and whose best attempt at a hook was ruining a much better Nine Inch Nails one, interpolating transgressive nineties crossover hit 'Closer' for the chorus of 'Hot Dog'. Trent Reznor was charmingly forgiving when asked about it:

'It's one thing if you know your place; like, "Hey, I'm an idiot who plays shitty music but people buy it—fuck it, I'm having fun,"' he would tell *Kerrang!* 'But it's another thing when you think you're David Bowie after you've stayed up all night to write a song called "Break Stuff". I mean, Fred Durst probably spelt the word "break" wrong the first couple of times. Fred might be a cool guy; I don't know him. But his "art"—in the word's loosest sense—sucks.'

The fact that Limp Bizkit got handed the keys to the *Mission Impossible* theme tells you a lot about where music was at the turn of the millennium. 'Take A Look Around' ended up being the lead single that would ultimately help inflate the Durst Hindenburg. It was the first track I ever downloaded illegally on Napster, a piracy attempt that took three tries because our internet was on the same line as our home phone, which meant that when our parents picked up to call someone our p2p progress bar stopped dead. A constant scene in our house would be me or David trying to covertly steal music while yelling at my dad to get off the phone, a fact made sweeter when he took a call from Universal Pictures and ended up as the official set doctor for *Mission Impossible II*, shot in and around Sydney, with its opening title music written by Limp Bizkit.

Of the many things that set Linkin Park apart from their contemporaries they are often lumped in with is the fact that they rarely ever swore. Their first album which raised so much ire with parents across the world didn't even come with a language warning, practically unheard of during the Y2K music boom. The worst it got, really, was Chester screaming 'Shut up when I'm talking to you!' on their breakout single 'One Step Closer'. When one stops to consider that he's probably yelling this at his id in the midst of existential torment, it's certainly more nuanced than Durst's early catchcry of 'Give me something to break / How 'bout your fuckin' face?'

Honestly, if the phrase 'toxic masculinity' had existed in 2001, Limp Bizkit's label would probably have found a way to use it to sell more albums.

* * *

Do not blame my generation for being confused. We came of age in an era where music went from being locked in shrink-wrapped jewel cases mostly out of our pocket-money price range to streaming out of the internet like water. We had

*NSYNC and Bloodhound Gang topping the charts in the same year, and Britney and Slim Shady denying having sex with each other at the MTV awards. Absolutely nothing made sense, which is why Fred Durst—a chubby Tyler Durden from North Carolina who knew when to carpe diem the shit out of an industry on the verge of existential collapse and ride that motherfucker straight into the apocalypse—found such success.

Where Linkin Park was driven by genuine pain, Limp Bizkit were primarily powered by aggression. Durst's unheralded talent was realising the power of offense as offence. A standard show involved veiled incitements to riot, to beat the living shit out of your fellow concertgoer, and to serve it to any girl that rebuffed your advances. It still amazes me that anyone with oestrogen listened to Limp Bizkit at all. Of all their contemporaries, their misogyny was the most rampantly consistent. Returning again to Eminem, who famously threatened to kill his own mother and ex-wife on every other song: even he didn't quite achieve the level of malice Durst reserved for his former lovers.

Violence, whether implied or actual, was fundamental to nu-metal lore. You only have to look at footage from Woodstock '99, possibly the biggest cultural disaster to befall America's youth in decades—where fans tore up scaffolding, set structures on fire and pummelled security for fun—to get a flavour of it. Much of my teens was spent being pinballed and thrashed about in similarly crazy mosh pits for hyper-aggressive bands like Slipknot and System of a Down, where 'circles of death' would open spontaneously and dudes would run at each other with the express desire of injuring one another like some modern gladiatorial contest. More often than not this directive came from the stage. Slipknot in particular made an art form out of hurting each other. It was thrilling and terrifying to watch. Limp Bizkit perfected this both on record and on stage as a soundtrack to hordes of adolescent boys getting completely out of control. Nu-metal is the reason Australian concert promoters eventually instated a 'D Barricade' as standard across music festivals, after a young Limp Bizkit fan, Jess Michalik, died of heart failure in an over-crushed pit.

Anything could happen.

Given this, as well as a constant backdrop of broken homes, addiction and abuse that shadowed many of the major players in nu-metal, it's reasonable to expect that violence would follow its way into its members' lives. The 2000s history books are littered with stories of death and accidental overdoses, with some bands having multiple members die on them in the space of a few years. Speedballs and pills, heart attacks and shootings: it does not make for soothing bedtime reading. But Linkin Park is the only group of this specific era where a frontman has occasioned such physical violence upon himself that it ended his life. In this respect, Bennington sits in closer proximity to tortured grunge legends like Kurt Cobain and Chris Cornell. I often wonder what my dad would have made of my anguish at Bennington's suicide—would he have declared moral victory at the inevitable endgame of one of the progenitors of the wrist-slitting music he so despised? Or perhaps he'd have seen something of himself in the devastating headlines, also understanding that the music was a way to process that despair, and offered solace.

Linkin Park eventually won the war of popular opinion, but thanks to Limp Bizkit it was a Pyrrhic victory; the second decade of the band's existence was spent experimenting with anything that could help them paper over the cross that had been painted in blood above their doors. That's because nu-metal, unlike other sonic subcultures from the same era, like emo or SoundCloud rap, is not looked upon favourably by the next generation. Any attempts at a renaissance have been lukewarm at best, with milestone retrospectives only serving to further deride every band associated with this genre as the worst thing to ever happen in popular music. Ten years on, popular noughties emo outfit, Paramore, is popping up as a key reference point for stadium pop acts like Olivia Rodrigo, but that kind of red carpet is not being rolled out for Limp Bizkit's DJ Lethal, John Otto or Wes Borland. We don't hear the hottest bands in the world citing Papa Roach as inspiration. Surely Linkin Park were aware of this movement in the tide even as they were coasting it towards record-shattering sales. Innovators to the end, they really started pushing the boat out on their third album and never looked back, trying new arrangements, radically different styles and bringing in unlikely collaborators. It was an experiment of diminishing returns, but it was part of the band's definitive plan to become bigger than the scene that seemed to follow them wherever they went. Chances are they'd be keener on British electronic star Rina Sawayama, who derided the insidious elements of the nu-metal genre while simultaneously blending its aesthetics into her writing, than anyone actively embracing it.

It's really only in light of Bennington's suicide, the sort of tragic occurrence we have now been conditioned to associate with innate genius, that Linkin Park managed to shake off the hyper-masculine yoke Durst had inadvertently tightened around every guitar band within range for years. Overnight, a band that many hadn't thought about since their cars got Bluetooth functionality entered a pantheon reserved for the kind of act you see on bootleg t-shirts in street stalls from Camden Market to Khao San Road. That this happened in the same year the notion of genre broke down for good, a potent combination of streaming and TikTok atomising 'taste' into billions of untraceable particles, certainly helped. Finally, Linkin Park could be whatever we wanted them to be: unmoored from association and repackaged as a defining rock band at the end of its hero's journey. Instead of being associated with irascible drudge merchants like Drowning Pool, Godsmack and Staind, Linkin Park was left with a very different legacy.

You don't have to understand Linkin Park to understand why they are so enduring.

In their own way, Limp Bizkit did that for us.

FOURTEEN

My dad jabbed steroids into Beyoncé's butt when she lost her voice the day of her stadium show. My dad jumped into Sydney Harbour to save my brand-new red Power Ranger toy. My dad had a friend who was a mad collector who owned more than 200 pinball machines and six MG convertibles. My dad made his own jam, muesli and sourdough bread. My dad bought me the Arnold Schwarzenegger guide to gaining muscle and shredding fat—when I was eleven.

My dad was a Toastmaster, helping complete strangers conquer their fear of public speaking. My dad was a close confidant of Martin Sharp, the psychedelic Australian artist who designed album covers for Cream and Hendrix. My dad protected me from cockroaches, but he never, ever killed them. My dad once covered for so many of my demerit points that he lost his own licence and had to ride a bicycle to work for a year.

My dad didn't know how to pray, but insisted on putting mezuzah up on my door when I moved into my first apartment. My dad laughed uproariously at *The Goon Show* on ABC radio. My dad came into my room one time when I was fourteen, dumped a stack of condoms he'd been given for free at a medical conference on my desk and left. My dad would crack open the bones of a chicken carcass and slurp out the marrow.

My dad was always mowing the lawn, even when it was already done. My dad was the doctor on set for *Candy*, where he helped teach Heath Ledger how to convincingly 'inject' heroin, knowledge based on a lifetime working with addicts. My dad tended a worm farm near the compost bins in our back garden. My dad had no time for bougie brands, for pointless things. My dad was a pioneering advocate of harm minimisation policy, fighting successive governments to ensure addicts received treatment rather than facing jail time, HIV/AIDS or death. My dad ate the whole apple: core, pips and all.

My dad was the preferred physician of Randall 'Animal' Nelson, the former bikie who delivered toys to sick kids at St Vincent's and drew *Looney Tunes* cartoons for his friends. My dad once jumped out of a still-moving car to avoid finishing a fight with our mum. My dad's ear for accents was second to none; he could impersonate anyone, particularly his own patients. My dad didn't believe in boardshorts, only Speedos.

My dad worked in the Cross for more than thirty years, but only installed a panic button during the ice epidemic after a patient tried to kill him. My Dad probably picked up an STI travelling around Greece in the seventies. My dad said Beyoncé's security guard was as wide as a refrigerator but had a heart of gold. My dad saw R.M. Williams boots as the height of fashion. My dad and I had the same size feet.

My dad once signed on to treat all of Thai Airways' stewardesses, many of whom were actually very pretty stewards. My dad convinced my mum to leave her fiancé and marry him, and that fiancé later became a billionaire. My dad was an in-demand public speaker at doctors' conferences, where he evangelised the importance of general practitioners looking after their own mental health.

My dad came to every one of my gigs, including the really bad ones. My dad's father abandoned his family in the snow fields when he was a child and my dad never skied again. My dad probably dated all of Mum's friends at some point, but we didn't talk about it.

My dad's snoring could level buildings. My dad let me play gory video games like *Duke Nukem* and *Return to Castle Wolfenstein*, but put a ban on watching *South Park*. My dad probably didn't want four kids. My dad once attended an emergency school meeting when kids were caught selling weed and was the only one to stand up and fight the principal on the outcome. My dad favoured rehabilitation over recrimination.

My dad always picked up other people's litter on the beach. My dad hated rushing holidays. My dad was happiest drinking coffee at a neighbourhood local, shooting the shit with people he'd only just met. My dad once didn't talk to his mother for nearly three years. My dad frequently brought the wrong fruit home from the markets, but never forgot flowers.

My dad took his own life on July 25, 2013.

FOURTEEN (WAIT, I'M NOT DONE)

. . . but really, the easiest shortcut to knowing my father, because you can't now, is Robin Williams. Picturing Robin Williams gets you three-quarters of the way there: a brilliant, effervescent and erudite man with so much body hair it covers his knuckles, wrists, back and toes; someone with an instant familiarity and ease with anyone, from the woman begging on the corner to the guy running the country; a man with a pitch-perfect ear for accents and smiling eyes diverting attention from the bilious clouds lingering behind them. Many think they have famous facsimiles, but Williams, in all his wild, hairy, hilarious glory, is it for my father. Nobody else comes close.

Like Dad, and his dad, I'm a very hairy person. My eyebrows weren't plural until I was eighteen. I had a thick moustache at eleven and was desperate to shave, scared of being teased. Dad took me to one of his patients, Ignazio, the Italian barber who worked next to a safe injecting room in Kings Cross, to have it waxed instead.

'Start shaving now,' he warned, 'and that's it for the rest of your life.'

Having this level of body hair coverage not seen since seventies *Cleo* spreads makes for a different type of existence. Unless we're in company, none of the men in my family sleeps with clothes on—or wears a shirt around the house. Coated with fine fur all year round, an eternal lanugo that is both a blessing and a burden, we are naturally a few degrees warmer than the average person.

Do not talk to my sister about body hair. She had it all nuked away as soon as she could ask for it. Even as an adult, she finds the entire notion nauseating. Mum? I guess she's gotten used to it spreading across all the men in her life, but you'll also never see her anywhere near a bathroom drain.

That heat doesn't stop at body temperature. Seidlers, but in particular Seidler boys of any generation, are hot-blooded. We feel things intensely and often. Confrontation is not something we shy away from, whether with one another, extended family, friends, colleagues or authority figures. This heat regularly manifests itself as indignation, which was certainly the case with Dad. Much of his life was spent eloquently and persistently arguing against those who thought heroin addicts were scum that only deserved death or prison. In letters, on television, at conferences, during dinner parties or on the street, Dad railed against small-mindedness, unsound policy, capital-G government. Half the time he was so charming it wouldn't even feel like a fight was on.

That heat was baked in from an early age. This may have been the reason he only succumbed to deep bouts of the blues every few years when I was a child. It seemed like it was just too bright in there, too hot for anything pernicious to survive long term.

* * *

Like tabby cats or certain species of dog, when you live with a hairy person you find pieces of them everywhere. We shed unconsciously, showers and kitchens and gardens and cars carrying residue of us that falls off and is reborn each day. Perhaps aware of this, Dad was militant about haircuts and hygiene. He'd grab our hands over lunch, lament the length of our nails and drag us out back to chomp at them with his shiny silver clippers. A reservoir of knowledge and myths, one of his favourites was that our hair and nails kept growing after we died (something he knew wasn't strictly true), which is why we Seidler boys, in our hairiness, really needed to keep on top of that kind of thing.

When Dad hit his mid-forties he acknowledged the brutal reality of his hairline, gave up on the barber and started shaving his own head. A few years later it wasn't uncommon to find Mum in the garden running a weapons-grade Wahl all over his shoulders and back. We liked to call this 'shearing'. Like Bruce Willis after *Die Hard 3*, Dad had adopted a laissez-faire attitude to hair. Everything became fair game. After a lifetime accumulating that coarse black human moss, it suddenly felt like he couldn't divest himself of it fast enough.

I often wonder if he clipped his fingernails and toenails on the morning he decided to kill himself. How much of the hair from his tremendous baboon chest shook free as he sucked in air for the last time. You don't need to pull at body hair to loosen it. It slides free simply through the act of being.

Mum sold our family home a few years after he passed away. There still would've been hair hiding everywhere.

FIFTEEN

There's nothing to talk about. She hibernates for two years, maybe even three. You might try and stop by on the off chance she'll come to the door and let you hover near the entry hall. On that rare occasion, you might catch a glimpse of her before she evaporates right before your eyes, descending so many levels beneath herself that skin is all there is. Debbie's here one minute, gone the next. It's a horrible magic trick. That's what well-wishers never fully appreciate about these types of deaths: two people die, even if only one of them stops breathing.

She can't tell if she's more mortified than she is devastated, the pair of emotions paralysing her in place. It's embarrassing, though she'll never say as much outright, to be a widow at such a young age, much less to suicide. This falling branch of the decision tree is what pins other people to the ground, but surely not Debbie Seidler. She has always been in control, neatly sidestepping the ills of everyday life by leaving very little to chance. It seems almost unreal that it has happened, even though the roadmap was always right there in front of her. Maybe she didn't believe it was possible, or she didn't believe that anyone could pull such a fast one on her. This is highly irregular. It's Debbie, not Ray, who always followed directions and meticulously planned ahead. So, no. She didn't believe it then and she still doesn't now.

All that's real is the searing sense of shame, crackling like an exposed shoulder that's spent too long in the sun. It's an intense burn, one that festers beneath the surface and radiates fiercest at night, keeping her awake as she lies in a bed that still retains the indent of her husband who she refuses to believe is not coming home.

Always twenty years younger in her looks, she feels like her biological age is finally catching up with her all at once. That everyone is witnessing her wizening before their very eyes: the belle of Bellevue Hill, that drop-dead knockout at Camp Cove beach, immortalised in black and white, holding an ice-cold can of Coca-Cola as she basks in the glow of a seemingly endless youth, is at long last wilting. Debbie Tate, the bachelorette suitors quarrelled over, the chalet ski queen; old, pathetic, alone . . .

Pathetic. It's the state of being Debbie most detests; to be waited on, fussed over, useless, pitied. In addition to always planning ahead, she prides herself on being no-nonsense, solutions oriented. This becomes a philosophical quagmire when faced with a rare problem she cannot solve. And so Debbie stops trying. She stays inside. She cries mostly in private. Prepares the same batch-cooked meals for five as she once did for six, mostly ignoring the fact that two of her adult sons should be returning to their adult lives. As Debbie sleepwalks through this period of her life, she mostly lives in a powder-blue dressing gown. It must have some trace elements of her husband on it; nobody ever sees it go into the wash.

Her children hate this dressing gown more than anything. It's stasis masquerading as comfort, an invincibility cloak they know they'll never prise Debbie back out of. She mooches around their house looking more like a mental patient than their father ever did. His wardrobe remains untouched—they are assured this is not unusual—and she sleeps next to one of his shirts every night, trying to summon him back. It's not obvious to anyone if this is a phase of grieving or will simply go on forever. In the early months not only is there no light at the end of the tunnel, but it often seems like Debbie is adamant on being the only one inside it. Her sorrow takes up all the oxygen; to let anyone else in would mean certain death.

Nobody is suggesting she rush through this period, of course. She has lost a life partner about three decades earlier than expected. It is chest-crushing stuff, especially for her parents, who had adopted Ray as their own since he and

Debbie married. Tibi and Vera embody the no-nonsense approach that has become their daughter's trademark, so for them this is particularly difficult to grapple with. Their generation is the one that Got On With It, picking up the shattered fragments of their lives in spite of tremendous horror, forging forward. Suicide is a particular affront to war survivors like my grandparents and their friends, many of whom have seen and lost it all. That it could happen to such a beautiful family in this, the best country in the world, is unthinkable. With no tools to process it—offers of psychological counselling advanced primarily to the young—Debbie's parents cope with this stunning gut-punch with the time-honoured technique of denial.

'The sky is blue,' Vera remarks to her grandsons as they leave the extra wake Debbie has had to call for all of Ray's patients and friends in Kings Cross—junkies and celebrities alike holding court on Darlinghurst Road. It is the only thing she'll say on the matter, a metaphor that's at once comforting and totally out of bounds. It's a variation of Get On With It, the only type of love Debbie's parents know how to dispense unconditionally.

Their implication here is crystal clear, though nobody dares utter it around Debbie during the Powder-Blue Gown period (at least not directly): it's time to get back out there. There is no such concept as Too Soon for post-Holocaust Austro-Hungarians, well-versed in replanting amputated family trees from piles of ash. What is she going to do? they implore their grandchildren over covert coffee dates, far from the prying ears and eyes of the community. Flop around that house forever? They are razor-focused, almost clinical in this mission. She doesn't need more time, they say. She needs a partner. What's done is done. She can't be like this. It isn't right.

Quite content to be like this forever, Debbie nonetheless senses the tide of popular opinion starting to shift. Pathos is slowly being replaced with frustration—first from her parents, but also, eventually, her children. If she had the wherewithal she would be outraged. The nerve, she mutters to herself, as she sits in Ray's home office, methodically making her way through the mess of the practice's accounts. Who are they to judge her? When were they given permission to decide it was time for her to move on? Was she even consulted? Bullshit. Debbie plays with the ratty cord on her sky-blue dressing gown, silently stewing.

* * *

I can't tell you when Mum crawls out of it. There's a murk in the years between, a swamp where memory is held under or simply lost. What I do recall is when she starts fighting back. We're squabbling over roast potatoes at the dining table that's still missing a head and she raises her voice, something I haven't heard her do in about eighteen months. Someone has been trying to set her up—there was an avalanche of suitors in those early months after Dad's passing—and she's not having it. Sudden anger was usually Debbie's natural default, her pleasure zone, and I can feel her settling back into it, albeit precariously. Mum is telling us to fuck off out of her business. She will meet someone when she is good and ready. All of these men are old and sad and pathetic. They are nothing like our father. She does not need to give them a chance—she already knows. She always knows. It doesn't matter that this one flew up from Melbourne, or that one bought her a thoughtful gift. Just fucking leave it alone, she is saying, pushing her green beans around the plate, it's my life.

Not only has Mum started showing up to dinner and eating, but she's come with opinions. From a seemingly impervious fog of grief, Mum emerges firing on all cylinders, ready to give it to anyone: friends, family, therapists. It's come a bit late in the textbook version of the seven stages, but Mum never met a rule she couldn't bend. Her anger swallows the depression, and it's all not quite fitting in, chunks of rage and sadness splutter all over the meatloaf.

The constant combat is exhausting for all of us, but we have to admit it's better than the mute ghost that preceded it. Through dogged resistance we can feel her coming back to life.

Dating is one thing, but Mum's heavy artillery is saved for conversation about The Conversation. Since Ray died, there's been an unspoken ban on discussing the circumstances of his death with the outside world. Many of our close friends still don't know exactly what happened. (Actually, they probably do, but since we're not allowed to talk about it, neither are they.) We are all complicit in the Great Denial, a phenomenon passed down two generations. But this confection is starting to grate, most notably for Zac, who is en route to a Master's in Clinical Psychology that will focus on men's mental health and suicide. Rather than move past grief, Zac has instead elected to make it a cornerstone of his professional life, and he is the first to start pushing back, accusing Mum of raising a family of hypocrites. It's a simple but devastating argument that Zac, foreshadowing a successful media career, knows is very difficult to come back from.

'How are we supposed to help others,' he says, trying to land the checkmate, 'if we can't even address it ourselves? Who else is going to help shift the needle on suicide if not those directly affected?'

Mum's not having a bar of it. It's no one else's fucking business. Her husband is but a few years gone, and now the Great Unwashed wants to rifle through our dirty laundry? Not a chance. She forbids it, threatening to turf Zac from the house. They bicker and we watch, trying to pick the right side while knowing that it's a stalemate. Instead of moving forward under the heavy fire, Mum begins to retreat again.

Zac catches sight of the dressing gown again at noon a few days later, and relents.

* * *

When Zac finally does utter the 'S' word in public, he does so in print. It's five years after Dad has died and Mum has sold the house, including the bed they shared for more than 30 years, the wardrobe full of his groovy shirts and straight-up Levi's, along with the tattered, indigo hammock out back where he lay with us as kids, singing us Louis Armstrong as we swung back and forth together on endless summer evenings. By now, Zac has upgraded his Master's to a PhD, won a university medal and started working for Movember. He is the guy media and corporations go to when they need someone to talk about men, masculinity and attitudes towards mental health, especially if you want someone under the age of 60 who presents well on camera. Inspired by his father, in spite of the temporary indignation of his mother, Zac has transformed tremendous tragedy into a career. He is becoming the Chester Bennington of psychology. I am in awe of him, as well as being slightly terrified and occasionally jealous. The heavy stuff we have worked so hard to put behind us? He is electing to sit with every day. 'Men do seek help for depression,' reads his headline in *The Guardian*. 'I wish my dad had.'

* * *

A year later, on the other side of the world, I begin writing this book. It first comes to me on holiday in Corfu, one of the many islands in Greece that Dad cavorted around in the 1970s, staying in different beds each night and quietly picking up herpes instead of the tab at the tavernas. I sit on a balcony overlooking the beach, surrounded by luridly pink bougain-villea, iridescent under the baking sun. I don't worry about Mum reading what I write because I don't ever expect to finish it. Maybe it's the heat, or the high salt content in every meal I eat, but Dad seems omnipresent. He's out the front of the apartment we're renting, tending to the overgrown flowers; on the beach, sitting in the clear, warm water in his Speedos, teaching me how to swim in my boxy orange floaties; laughing with the waiter at the Lord Byron, eating a whole fish doused in oil and lemon, head, bones and all.

Mum calls me on the last day of my holiday. She sounds nervous, like she's got something awful she needs to get out that she feels sick holding on to. As she's going through the motions of asking me irrelevant questions about the island and my flight home to London, I soon realise what's eating her. She's finally met someone.

I listen to her talk, noting my palpable relief when she finally lets it out. Mum is trepidatious but excited; after a bit of a shaky start, this new relationship seems to be moving positively. She sounds ten years younger. They're spending a lot of time together, starting to do standard couple things.

They have dinner together a few nights a week, sometimes go to the movies when they can find a film they both agree on. Mum says that she hasn't introduced him as her partner to her friends yet, as most of them know him and she doesn't want them to judge.

'Wait,' I interrupt, walking down the hill to the water in the clay-oven heat. 'Judge you, or judge him? And why does it matter?'

'You know,' Mum replies, sighing across continents. 'People like to gossip.'

Mentally, I rifle through my laundry list of appropriate responses: 'Who cares?', 'Let them talk', 'They're not worried about you', 'Ignore them' and 'People only really care about themselves'. I recognise many of these are stock answers Dad gave me a decade ago, when I fretted about people finding out I was depressed. It would seem strange to be re-dispensing this advice to my 58-year-old mother, but it wouldn't be, really. Shame, and our intrinsic fear of it, is multi-directional, generational and age-agnostic. We are coming out the other side of one of the most terrible events that can befall a family, and we remain steadfastly in its thrall. It must be our peoples' legacy to feel terrible and happy at the same time—for the rest of time. When Ray married my mum, he stomped on a glass, signifying the destruction of the Jewish Temple some 2000 years prior, warning us that sweet and sour memories will always be bound in a double helix. Now, shame conversely dictates that we shouldn't experience joy in the wake of such a huge loss, nor remain mired in tragedy when the sky outside is so blue.

'Mum, you should see the beach here,' I say, changing the subject. 'The water is incredible but the whole shoreline is covered in rocks. You can't walk on it without thongs.'

'That's the price you pay for a European summer, honey. Are they charging you for a chair?'

'Yeah, but it's only like ten euros a day.'

'Could be a lot worse,' she says. 'In Italy I remember it was three times as much. Sorry, I just remembered, you wanted to tell me about a new piece you were writing?'

The red notebook in my bag is nearly out of pages. I've been writing for hours every day, paragraphs rushing like blood. It's coming out not as fragments but nearly fully formed. Like it was always there. Sleep seems irrelevant; I try for a few hours and then give up and head back to the desk. There's only a hairline between creativity and tripping out of control, but I've dealt with that balance long enough to know I'm on the right side of it. I've never been so sure of something in my life.

'Oh yeah, don't worry,' I say. 'If it actually turns into something, I'll let you know.'

SIXTEEN

Kanye West wasn't totally wrong when he called bipolar disorder a superpower. This phenomenon of seeing invisible, connecting pieces come together that don't even sit in the same puzzle box—that's real. He just forgot to mention the other bits.

I'll never forget receiving my diagnosis. It took less than fifteen minutes. Dad had wrangled the appointment with one of the more pre-eminent psychologists in the country, which was very difficult to procure. The office was large and imposing. The professor had a nose like a hawk and a similar demeanour. He'd already consulted my case file, and I sat cowering in the corner as he circled me, firing off questions. Little about that traumatic afternoon at the institute struck me as the makings of a Marvel origin story.

In Westian philosophy, bipolar is a superpower not in the sense that it taps into a new skill, but rather that once you take off it optimises an existing skill so intensely that the edges start to shimmer. In this sense, I know what he means. When I'm elevated and there's a pen nearby, ideas drop into the slot and the arcade game in my subconscious hums to life. It glows and pulses like a neon sign that I fly by on a dark Parisian street. Hidden mysteries emerge in a complex harmony that's utterly perfect but frustratingly difficult to explain. Not that I didn't try.

I'm not racing. I'm just excited.

Do you remember where you were when Kanye dropped 'All of the Lights'? How it made you feel? The critics called it 'maximalist'. That's a word deployed by someone to describe a sensation they can feel but can't understand. Whenever I hear this song I am taken by its manic beauty. The frankly staggering process behind its creation. They said it was all-encompassing. Symphonic. Unparalleled in its vision. A 'magnificent high'. And indeed, 'All of the Lights' is all of these things. It is also the by-product of being phenomenally, catastrophically Up.

There are fourteen additional voices on 'All of the Lights'. That line-up includes Elton John, Rihanna, Charlie Wilson, John Legend, La Roux, The-Dream, Kid Cudi, Alicia Keys, Drake and, still inexplicably, a full rap verse by Fergie of The Black Eyed Peas. The arrangement is a fever dream; it lays waste to poor-quality headphones. There are so many layers of backing vocals on it, all blended together with such ferocity that it can be difficult to pick out which superstar singer you're actually hearing. 'All of the Lights' is exactly what the inside of my head looks like when I can't come down; bombastic, free-associating and helmed by a conductor wearing purple kicks that hasn't slept more than a few hours a night in the last ten days.

I heard 'All of the Lights' very early on in the *My Beautiful Dark Twisted Fantasy* campaign. The label had sent me an advance copy, the kind you used to get with big FBI warnings slapped all over it. It was 2010, and instead of helping Dad in the garden I was stopped in the middle of my street with my headphones on, suddenly blinking back tears. My internal thermometer couldn't make up its mind; a minute ago I'd been shivering, now I felt sweat pooling in my jeans. I had recognised something deeper in this modern parable about the pitfalls of fame. Kanye was still two albums and as many name changes away from being able to articulate exactly what it was, but I knew.

That gorgeous, volatile superpower.

'All of the Lights' is a song that took two years to write and two months to finish. Rihanna got the call to do her vocals at two in the morning. Much of it was recorded in Hawaii, but West wasn't there for a holiday. He'd exiled himself after a miscalculated display of bravado at an awards ceremony had blown up spectacularly in his face. A pattern in the outbursts not yet established, a diagnosis not yet procured, West, still smarting from being labelled a 'jackass' by the first Black president of the United States, promptly disappeared.

Nobody creates good work when they are depressed. The myth of the tortured artist is just that. You don't manifest brilliance like Jeff Buckley or Nick Drake when in the throes of a Down episode. No musician records intricate orchestral pieces when they can't even get themselves out of bed to face the mirror. If mania is the turbo boost, then depression is the brick wall you slam into at high speed continually. If art floats, retains any sense of buoyancy, this is a balm self-applied after the agony stops. It emerges in spite of it, not because of it.

I understand this now.

Depression is nothing. It is a feeling of nothingness, to the point where I cannot tell you a single thing I have said or done over the multiple protracted periods of it in my adult life. The stories of my behaviour are Midrash, commentary, observations. They are passed down to me by my family, friends, ex-lovers. Depression is a fugue state in which nothing is achieved aside from the eventual decision to get better, which is not one that anyone else in your life can truly force upon you.

Though Kanye appears stupendously prolific, he must also be accustomed to this sensation. There must be periods where he flames out, burning through all the nitrous that's kept him achieving at such a high level and shuts down. We hardly ever hear about this. For the most part, hip-hop and mental health go about as well together as its track record with homosexuality. Kid Cudi, Kanye's musical next-of-kin, has been far more upfront. 'Sadness eats away at me sometimes,' he wrote in 2016, before checking himself into a facility to get help.

Of course, we know Kanye also gets sad. Fifteen years on from her passing he is still grieving the loss of his mother. When he feels misunderstood by his peers or the public he tends to process this shame by exiling himself—to Honolulu, to Paris, to Wyoming. Kanye is such a singular, exuberant overachiever that he has no poker face. When he's down, when he's hurting, it's impossible not to see it. There is an entire corner of the internet dedicated to this.

* * *

I was prescribed lithium a decade ago and it's been the only medication that's stuck. Like bumpers in a bowling alley, it hovers around the outer limits of my mood, protecting me from descending too low or catapulting too high. Though my quality of life is immeasurably better, I can't help but feel like this chemical padding muffles the more glimmering parts of my self-expression. Whenever I have writer's block, or can't communicate a concept, I return to the professionals to state my case. I need to access the highs to get this work done, I wind up explaining in some variation to a concerned doctor, psychologist or psychiatrist, but I also can't live with them. There has to be another way, a different configuration of pills. Some of the things I've done while I've been Up you won't even believe. The stealing, the lying, the fucking, the drugs, the violence. I'm not sure I even believe it. It's an honest-to-God miracle I'm not in jail. Do you know one night I lay down in the middle of a four-lane road just to see if a car would stop? I was already stable; they were tranquillising me every night. I was 22. What happens when I'm 42? My dad will not be there to save me anymore.

Bipolar is a superpower, but these superpowers need management. Sometimes it's like I can't press the eject button as the Batmobile is about to crash into a skyscraper; other times I can't even find the energy to get into the suit. There is a difference between accessing stardust and living on another planet. At some point those of us lucky enough to have dealt with this pinball personality long enough realise how to flag when the rocket looks like it might be leaving Earth. We know we have to use it sparingly, lest we inadvertently burn the atmosphere around us. West said it himself to David Letterman: 'This is like a sprained brain, like having a sprained ankle. If someone has a sprained ankle, you're not going to push on him more.'

Kanye West ran for President in 2020, which is honestly something I have considered a good idea at various points in my life. By that point his diagnosis was out there, his even-more-famous wife was pleading for compassion, and it was hard to know where to look. It felt like the wheels were coming off from one of the most innovative musicians of his era; everywhere you turned there were sparks fizzing out as metal grated against steel. Kanye had lost control of his suit. His politics veered so far right they ended up in oncoming traffic; having once declared that as a Black man he could buy his way out of jail but he couldn't buy freedom, Kanye was now on air saying slavery was 'a choice'. At one point he broke down during a rally, plainly terrified of the position he'd found himself in, and it was captured by an attendee and beamed around the world. The Sad Kanye meme suddenly wasn't funny anymore. It was horrific.

When I was diagnosed at 21, bipolar wasn't presented to me as a superpower, but a disorder. A disaster, even. I started psychiatry sessions within the year, only after I cycled through all of the dud therapists that somehow managed to make me feel worse than I already did. Everyone cast bipolar as some-thing wrong with me; it needed to be monitored, adjusted and continuously refined to bring this alleged chemical imbal-ance back to normal. I bristled, I fought back, but eventually I did what I was told. There will be no Grammy Awards or Pulitzers in my future. I will probably never call a key collaborator at two in the morning. Stability has ensured that

80 per cent of the time I lead an entirely regular and vastly uninteresting existence.

It's taken me a long time and more than a few deaths to realise that the definition of balance, like my definition of good work, is relative. There is a huge spectrum between out of control and passively existing. Though I embrace life with all the tools available to me, that last 20 per cent is uncomfortable. It is exhausting and it wears me out. But it is a gift. It is knowing you need fourteen backing vocalists, these specific people in this specific arrangement, without having to explain why. It is the reason Kanye West released 'All of the Lights' instead of giving it to another artist as he'd originally planned. There are three French horn players, two trombonists and a flautist on the track. A chorus of golden cornets offset Jeff Bhasker's driving synth bass line. It is quite literally bursting, so heavy with the weight of living life the way a bipolar superhero does. And yet, it soars.

* * *

This is not how people were trained to view my condition around the time we finally figured out what was going on with my uninhibited mood swings. Bipolar disorder was 'the new ADHD', Mum said. They were just handing out diagnoses willy-nilly, like orange quarters at half-time. You could tell she wasn't crash-hot on raising a young maniac. It was far easier to chalk my behaviour down to growing pains—after all, I hadn't acted out much as a teenager when compared to some of my friends.

After that appointment at the Black Dog Institute where I was first diagnosed, I stood shell-shocked at the gate, shaking uncontrollably, crying and unable to deal. Dad was out there with me, holding me close in his hairy bear arms, trying out different ways of consoling me. None of them were working. I wasn't having it. I was convinced that I was tainted forever; that I'd never get a stable job, find a wife, experience prolonged periods of happiness. I'd heard the stories, seen the movies. I knew what this shit was and what it meant for me.

Psychiatric disorders were approached very differently in 2008. I was actively encouraged by those around me to keep this new information to myself on the very real presumption such knowledge would impact my personal or professional life. While Kanye West was letting blood across *808s & Heartbreak*, my girlfriend at the time sat bolt upright in bed and walked out of the house when I told her what was wrong with me. It's almost unbelievable to imagine that now, when caring about mental health is so virtuous and such a monetisable cause for brands. Even depression was still on the fringe then, but bipolar was very much a no-fly zone.

Eventually I calmed down, though I can't remember how or why. Dad took me home and sat me down in front of the family PC, making sure I watched as he googled 'famous

people with bipolar disorder'. He couldn't have possibly antici-
pated the length and breadth of that list, which is probably
twice as long when you factor in the writers, actors, musicians,
designers, directors and cinematographers still not talking
about it. Say what you like about Kanye, the guy really kicked
that door wide open.

I love this memory: Dad and me in the upstairs study,
talking it out, stopping at detailed entries for Stephen Fry,
Virginia Woolf and Lou Reed. It's as if we're co-conspirators
in this secret club full of cool members with great ideas.
I'm wiping snot from my face and trying to focus on this,
ignoring the word 'disorder' blasting out from every Wiki
page. Most of these people are excellent, I reason. Surely it
can't be that much of a curse.

Dad's stressed out too, realising that I'm now officially more
like him than just our looks, and that this is going to take a
lot of work to get under control. I don't clock it at the time,
but when he looks at me he's not just seeing himself and the
depression that's been dancing around him since he was a
boy. He's also seeing his father. I can bet he's really fucking
regretting giving me Marcell as a middle name. Probably
thinks he's set this entire disaster on its course from eight days
old, the moment the mohel took my foreskin for safekeeping.

We don't talk about any of this. In fact, we never really
do. For now, Dad is protecting me as he always has, selflessly.
'See?' he said, scrolling past Jimi Hendrix, who once sang

that manic depression was searching his soul. 'Look at all these incredible people. Look at what they've achieved. It isn't a life sentence.'

Depending on your experience, the lights Kanye refers to can mean many different things. As he explains in the song, they can be oppressive, seductive, revealing or disarming. Those bright lights can be cameras, police cars, strobes, flashlights.

What's more difficult to approximate is the thin ring that hovers above your retina after the bulb flashes and the temperature dims. It's the imprint of a low that follows every high, serving as a silent warning. Blinding lights may be over in a matter of seconds, but living with bipolar means having to handle what comes next. We get the sense Kanye understands this. It's why he hands the last 30 seconds of 'All of the Lights' to Elton John who voices his angst: 'I tried to tell you, but all I could say was oh'. And just like that, the suit runs out of oomph; a mere man now falling helplessly through the sky.

To you, this change at first might be imperceivable. Much of this relies on whether you are endowed with a particular superpower that, for the briefest moment, lets you truly see everything.

SEVENTEEN

Dad's dead, but we can't kill his Twitter account. Now that he's passed on, Dr Ray is finally on the verge of something resembling minor celebrity, an unofficial goal of the back half of his professional life. Within hours of the news breaking, 140-character tributes start slowly trickling in from the internet contingent of Dad's bizarrely wonky Venn diagram of friends and fans, growing in pressure until a few days after Shiva is done, when the dam finally bursts. Former colleagues, current addicts, serious actors, frontmen finally gone clean, nurses, eccentric artists, aged-care workers, city officials, local sex workers, police officers, cantankerous Italian baristas and barbers, industry editors, international medical publications and family members we forgot were still alive all clamour for space in the mentions column of @drrayseidler, recalling his empathy, wit and greatest hits.

Dad loved to weigh in on stuff he knew loads about—like drug policy, harm minimisation or addiction medicine—but also shit that was not even in the slightest bit in his wheel-house. He wrote letters to the editor every other day and they were regularly published. This editorial verification was important to him, and Mum knew it. For decades, she had kept a bulging photo album full of his newspaper clippings, something she'd also fastidiously repeat for me once I became a journalist. Years later, I realised this sort of clerical work wasn't just to assuage the often-swollen Seidler male ego. To my knowledge Dad never asked her to do it, nor did he check on its maintenance. But these archives were crucial to Dad's recovery when he was depressed. Mum would pull out the heavy, plastic-lined tome and plonk it ceremoniously in front of her husband, standing over him as he sat slumped in his study.

Look, she'd say, turning page after page in front of his colourless eyes.

You did all of this.

You are important.

You are respected.

You are loved.

The discourse around decommissioning social media accounts of the dearly departed has only started gathering steam by the time Dad joins their ranks. By some estimates, there will soon be more ghosts hanging out on Facebook than people. These floating dead are still technically alive in the eyes of Silicon Valley, and so they stumble on, cryogenically suspended in code. It's becoming a serious issue, particularly for young people losing their mates prematurely to cancer or car accidents but finding themselves constantly being reminded of their presence in the feed. I get the luxury of witnessing this drama in real-time, as Mum is of the generation that does not yet see the need for a personal computer. Not only does she share a PC with her deceased husband, but also an email client, account and software. Naturally, Dad set up alerts for himself—ego is a dish best served automated—which means every time he's mentioned on the platform Mum's never used or heard of, she receives an email. This is not an ideal way to navigate grief, and somewhat explains the brusqueness with which she summons me into her bookkeeping shrine and formally requests that I Turn The Fucking Thing Off.

Another thing Mum and Dad shared were incredibly simple passwords, the kind Google would flat out reject today, named for his kids and almost always utilising the year I was born. Until recently, a simple variation on this combination could get you into our private bank and library accounts, Blockbuster, Medicare, voicemail inbox, front door code and credit cards. Nobody in our family has ever been locked out of anything secure for more than 30 seconds. It is the innocent age that starts in the mid-nineties, where phishing still requires a rod and tackle and everyone keeps seven years of receipts in a box for tax time.

But, lo and behold, the bastard's gone and done something different for his Twitter password. Nothing works: not string permutations, guesswork, l3tt3r-4-numb3r substitution, rAnDom CapiTaliSation, mashing the keyboard, reverse-engineering or screaming at the screen. Dad's public account has become infernally private and there seems to be sweet fuck-all I can do about it.

* * *

Strange thing, Twitter. Dad and I lived in the same house, ate the same Challah on Friday night, fought over the same patchy hot water between floors—'Oy, Princess! Some of us have to go to work!'—but had zero interactions online. True, I wouldn't have encouraged it on Facebook, let alone Myspace, MSN Messenger or mIRC, but Twitter is the marketplace of ideas, an agora in a world of walled gardens. It's the digital equivalent of running into Dad at a restaurant, sitting close enough to hear him tell one of his great, 90 per cent over-exaggerated stories but not stopping by his table to say hello. I am my father's son; it's certainly not the private life for me. By age 23 I'd already written about intense family holidays, my competitive relationship with my younger brother and my colourful sex life, and run a notorious blog that poked fun at my own religion. My and Dad's oscillating Twitter accounts represented the last vestige of distance between man and boy, one that was shrinking fast.

He asked me for help getting set up on Twitter and never consulted me again. Every so often, when I found myself in a heated, profanity-laced argument with an internet troll, or casually lambasting members of local or state parliament, I remembered that Dad followed 39 people on Twitter and one of them was me. I'd click over to his profile, which he hadn't locked, and see him proffering unsolicited opinions on a *New York Times* piece regarding hoarding. 'Long overdue, a mental illness which can destroy lives,' he'd note. I'm pretty sure he was talking about Mum.

* * *

'Can't you call someone?'

'Mum,' I say. 'You can't just *call* Twitter.'

I'm slouched helplessly in front of the screen and another mention pings through:

terrible news about @drrayseidler. helped me kick the gear in 92 and changed my life. a kind soul. RIP.

'Of course you bloody well can.' Mum's phone calls are the stuff of legend. She's never met a bureaucrat she hasn't convinced, cajoled or outright blackmailed to do her bidding. Mum could make late video return fees disappear. She can wipe $1000 off the price of a new car. She can get a censored book back onto the English syllabus. It is easy to understand why she thinks this should be a walk in the park.

'You can't.'

'You just don't want to try,' she says.

'Ordinarily true, but this time I'm not kidding.'

The inbox pings again. Fuck's sake.

I sigh. 'Alright, let me explain this one more time. Dad signed up for Twitter. He turned on email notifications in his settings. We can't turn them off unless we can get access to his account, which we can't, because for some unknown fucking reason this is the one time in his life he decided to change a password—'

'I think that might have been Andy,' she interrupts.

'Sounds about right.' Andy is our shit-for-brains IT guy who massacres more technology than he fixes. 'In any case, I doubt he would have told Andy what it was, so pending us getting hold of someone at this faceless global company with no office in the Southern Hemisphere, there's really only one option . . .'

'No,' she says firmly.

'Why not?'

'Because. If I get rid of them, they're gone. What if there's something important in there?'

'Mum, you can't keep a dead man's email inbox alive for posterity.'

'I'm not *doing* it!'

She's about to cry, I know it.

'Okay, okay. Well, for a start, we're going to put on an auto-responder and figure out a way to mute the notifications or divert them or something . . .'

'You're not going to—'

'No, I'm not going to delete anything, Mum.'

I've spent three weeks in complete business mode, dealing with affairs, organising multiple wakes, recalling siblings from overseas and writing obituaries to the point where I've pretty much forgotten that something terrible has happened in this very house. Meanwhile, Mum's been living every excruciating minute of it, and just as she's started to crawl back towards the light we have to deal with this tech-induced trauma.

'I'm sure someone at work can get put in touch with someone at Twitter,' I say softly, not entirely knowing if it's true. 'I'll call them tomorrow.'

* * *

By July 2013, Facebook's population is 1.1 billion, in effect making it the world's third largest country. That same year, about three million of those people will die. In a classic stitch-up, Dad doesn't use Facebook, which has been 'memorialising' accounts for a couple of years after users kept seeing their dead friends spewed up by an emotionless algorithm and campaigned to have something done about it. Had Dad opted for Zuckbook, there would have been an entire ecosystem set up for us to change his profile, even without knowing his logins. Sure, it's super weird to stay friends with a spirit, wishing them happy birthday each year like they give a shit, but given the alternative of following a zombie it doesn't seem like such an uninspired choice.

It turns out you can call Twitter. Contrary to my huffing and puffing, they'd recently set up an office in Sydney—their first this side of the equator—to help them in their ultimate mission of convincing brands to divert their large TV spends to online. An upbeat receptionist puts me through to a digital strategist, who patches me over to a client services lead, who yells across the open plan, Skittles-coloured office at the integrated experience manager, who usually ends up dealing with issues nobody else wants to.

I know that I'm being bumped up the chain under false pretences. I'm a small fry at one of the most decorated agencies in the country, but my job title has the word 'Social' in it. The people I work with come from the land of full-page print ads and 60-second TV spots that cost millions of dollars. They drink rosé on superyachts at the annual advertising awards in Cannes. None of these blokes would put money on Facebook even being around in two years. But clients won't leave them alone about it, so they christen me 'Social Copywriter', the adland equivalent of a mailroom kid they hope will melt quietly into the furniture. At our office I am invisible, but to Jessica, who presumably also had a title hoisted upon her by people who haven't quite figured out where she fits, I might be somebody.

Jessica says she can't access a deceased account without 100 points of legal proof that we are next of kin, but that once I send that over she'll be happy to help.

Mum is thrilled. The tap is going to be turned off. She wants to buy me lunch, temporarily forgetting I haven't seen the outside world since my birthday and have a beard thick enough to guarantee being pulled aside at an airport. She rushes off to tell the kids about the Twitter miracle while Jessica and I finalise the details on loudspeaker.

'Okay, so,' she says, phone to her chin as she types. 'Your documentation checks out, thanks for that. I'm going to go ahead and put in a request for all notifications on this account to be permanently turned off, but I did want to ask you, while we're here . . .'

I should have seen this coming. You don't get into the mainframe of the beast without the chance for a shot at its heart.

'Do I want to delete it?'

'Yes. We've found in the past this helps with closure; sometimes people come across their loved ones in a search or some other way and it can be very, um . . . triggering.'

I look down at the phone and think about Mum and her inbox full of her husband's emails, her mailbox stuffed with his voice messages. I think about moving on and honouring without forgetting. I look at Dad's battered R.M.s on my feet and realise that the seat I'm currently sitting in, with the sort of hunched-over posture he hated, is probably the seat he sat in when he decided to die. And then I think about all the positive encouragement I wish I'd tweeted him instead of wasting time glibly critiquing the second albums of bands I didn't even like.

'One second,' I say and log onto Twitter on the old PC, looking for @drrayseidler one last time.

My father's last post is date-stamped exactly two weeks before he died. Unsurprisingly, it's another opinion of an opinion, the sort of Midrash meta-commentary he loved. His final online output, tweeted out at 4.09 p.m., is a *Sydney Morning Herald* lifestyle article called 'The Art of Having Your Own Back'. Dad's appended the piece with one of his short notes, and now it runs right through me:

Ah compassion in short supply for us and our fellow humans.

All the thoughts I've been working overtime to bury start to force their way past the levee. It's suddenly, sickeningly clear to me that this one breadcrumb leads to many more I've missed—opportunities for intervention not taken seriously enough, or even noticed at all. Instinctively, I jump up to slam the door shut. I need to do this alone. Scrolling wildly through the feed, I try to assure myself that what I have found is not forming a pattern. I am making impossible connections, seeing things retrospectively that were never there in the first place. From nowhere, a torrent of questions that all start with 'What if . . .' flood my brain. I sit bent over the screen like a roulette wheel tipped on its side, spinning insatiably through the detritus of Ray's digital life, hoping not to land on anything overly portentous. In general, his posts seem innocuous; Dad alternately posts about the legalisation of marijuana, Iran, climate science. He makes a strange crack about the rapper Rick Ross looking good in a dressing gown. It's all nothing. But wait. Here's a *Salon* piece here titled 'I do not fear death'. False alarm, its author has terminal cancer. Another spin, where under a *New York Times* piece on mental illness, Ray bashes out another cryptic comment 'Grief is not depression. It is normal.' That could be something, right? I start to get the sense that I am sweating absolutely everywhere. It's all so thrilling—and pointless. What exactly am I chasing?

Anyone that tells you a suicide is an open-and-shut case has not had it happen to them. No matter your level of pragmatism or intellect, or whether you fully engage with mental health research or think it's all quackery, the result never changes. It's a never-ending Easter Egg hunt with no chocolate for anyone. The closest I'm going to get here is something shiny that looks like foil, a scrap of understanding, but is actually an illusion. Even so, this will not be the last time I scour Dad's digital scrapbook for clues. Each time I am called upon to console a friend who has had someone close to them take their own life, the impetus is identical. This desire to play detective, doggedly seeking resolution, instead of marinating in a grief that plainly offers none, is the same shameless optimism that has kept humans alive for millennia. Unyielding, ruinous self-belief that, with enough determination, we could have fixed it. I am looking for clues not because I want answers, but because I want hope, preferably in the form of unassailable logic to hold on to. It occurs to me that my family will all spend countless afternoons in this boundless garden over the years to come. Even if we find little, we'll keep searching, somehow compelled to find that one extra thing that will bind all the grief and confusion into something we can know and hold and understand.

'Jonathan?' Jessica says. The extended silence is freaking her out.

'No, I don't think I'll do that,' I say quickly, reconstructing my game face. I don't want Mum busting back into the room and catching me in such a state. Something is starting to burst beyond the wall I've hastily erected around myself and I'm not yet ready for that to happen around other people. 'Actually, I think I'd like to keep it.'

EIGHTEEN

If you are worried about something then write it down. Make a list of all the ways out, choose the best solution for tomorrow and plan just how you'll do it.

—from *Dr Raymond Seidler's Relaxation Tape*, 1991

NINETEEN

Two weeks after Shiva I sign up for yoga. It's more difficult than I imagine; what hurts the most are the simplest poses. At one point in my life I could bench press close to twice my body weight, but I can't hold a Downward Dog for longer than 30 seconds. Unlike lifting weights, which is easy to understand and simple to master, yoga is seemingly inscrutable. The mat is a blank canvas and I frequently forget to bring paints. Bereft of the courage to quit, and forced by circumstances to take time off work, I attend midday sessions with dark circles around my eyes, surrounded by perennially tanned mothers who run their own boutique candle businesses on the internet. Soaking in this cloistered space of privilege, incense and oestrogen, I eventually start flowing into it.

Our instructor is an aspiring actor and she sings like a goddess. I know I'm not meant to be here for Celeste's 'Om

Shanti' harmonies but her Warm Open remains one of the few comforts that linger after I walk out of the studio and into the whipping winter wind. Her hair is a mess of carrot-coloured ringlets and she has the sort of soothing tone that makes phrases like 'Open your heart eye and gaze inwards towards the universe' sound completely normal.

I wear gym shorts battered from years of sweat and ratty tank tops that barely cover my torso. Grieving affords me a hall pass to shabbiness and I lean into it. Celeste seems aware that I probably shouldn't be here at this time of day, not yet wealthy enough to opt out of the land of the living every Tuesday and Friday. She doesn't mention it, but at the end of each class I can feel it in the way she rubs my temples in slow concentric circles during meditation.

Mindfulness is a rich white person's way to describe zeroing in on a dull, repetitive set of actions meant to soothe the spirit, which at the outset is all yoga is. It's only in the midst of a particularly taxing pose called Pigeon, some five weeks into my membership, that I finally start to appreciate the way oxygen and blood sing and bubble across my body. My rusted glutes screech as I deliberately splay my limbs out in front of my torso, breathe and fold. A candle flickers, someone farts. The seconds drip into minutes.

It's not obvious at first that what I am actually here for is Shavasana. Initially, I write it off as a cool-down, an activity I treat with the same disinterest as a warm-up, just some extra credit you do when you're trying to be the gym teacher's pet. These quiet ten or so minutes at the end of practice are reserved for deep, internal breathing and contemplation. I find them exceptionally uncomfortable, not wanting to be alone with my thoughts, afraid to let them drift into dangerous corners or coalesce into something I'm yet to verbalise. But there's only so long I can spend in a headstand, and I've been sleeping fitfully for weeks, so it doesn't take much to succumb. Though the room is pungent and warm from movement, our bodies regulate temperature quickly. Celeste hums a tune of her own design as she covers us in thick grey blankets and encourages us to close our eyes.

The pose Shavasana requires is devilish in itself, a process through which I'm supposed to elegantly unfurl the anxious knots suffocating my brain. Mostly it involves me trying to tune out the obnoxious breathing of other people and drift into a temporary nap state. This experiment is not successful. One day after class, as all the mothers chatter and roll up their sweat-slicked mats, I ask Celeste to tell me what I'm doing wrong. She chuckles in the knowing way of someone who hasn't had high blood pressure since 9/11. 'Shavasana is a bit like a Magic Eye trick,' she explains. 'You can try really hard to see what's hiding in the patterns, but it's only when you trust yourself to relax your vision that you finally unlock what's behind them.'

I had a book of these autostereograms as a ten-year-old. This is sage advice.

The following session seems primed for me to put this technique to work. A large contingent of the annoying regulars aren't here today. We are blessed with space; there is nobody within swinging distance of my mat. I am positioned centre-left so that I can watch Celeste guide me through Warriors 1 and 2, which I always get confused even though they've been explained to me dozens of times. Everything is feeling just groovy, and as we collapse into Shavasana I become aware for the first time that I'm focused on absolutely nothing.

I see him suddenly through the blackness of my eyelids, so absurdly visceral that I almost want to laugh. Of course I would find him here, during meditation, an activity in which he tried fruitlessly to convince me to partake in for years while he was alive. He appears in continual flashes, vignettes of long-buried memory. He floats, as I do, somewhere not far in the distance, but I can feel him. His presence, his radiant heat, his hairy bulk. Held in the nothing, the pendulum of my childhood flicks left, then right. He is taking me for my first haircut. His big hands curl around mine as we wait to cross the road. He is clapping excitedly in time with my high school jazz band performance. He is mowing the lawn in the height of summer, in earmuffs and red undies, ankle guards around his boots. He is marshalling a Watsons Bay cul-de-sac, yelling that if I don't get back on that bike I'll never learn how to ride without training wheels.

And just when I think I've rinsed it all out: a quiet rupture from the deep. It materialises slowly; Dad and I are down the road, in the Seagull Room of Bondi Pavilion. It is a festival of yoga, and Oma is there too. It feels like I am here against my will, so I must be a teenager. Oma is espousing the virtues of this new-age junk, telling me she's been standing on her head since the sixties. A small gong rings at the front of the room and soon it is filled with Omms. I am squirming with embarrassment and this is the last straw. Storming out of shot, I hear Ray pleading with me. 'Come on, Jonathan! How do you know you won't like it if you don't even give it a chance?'

* * *

Shavasana quickly becomes an addiction. Soon I can access Dad within 30 seconds of going under, starting from a previously established memory before layering a glittering new one over it. As I meditate I collect visions of my father like collector cards, hungry to add them to my set. The visions gain depth and edge; faint at first, like they're trying to figure out what to be, before snapping with crystalline clarity.

But he is just a projection. I am summoning him, not bringing him back. Unsure how I feel about this, I decide to feel everything at once.

There's a refreshing absence of pretence in the subconscious. Every so often the vision of Dad flickers, a broadcast glitch. In the cavernous room of my mind I conjure up a more realistic hologram of my father: yanking open the door of our people-mover while Mum's driving us to synagogue for Yom Kippur and threatening to jump out; holding petty grievances against other doctors with higher media profiles; having epic, multi-year rows with his sister and mother. I squirm in the enforced darkness, trying to flick the dial back to Hero Dad, but the channel has disappeared.

Emerging into my final Namaste, I leave each session with wet tears baking my face, smiling. Celeste, noticing a pattern, begins to withdraw, allowing me the space. It's hard to blame her for being shocked when one afternoon, I sit bolt upright in the middle of meditation and hurry out of the room, moving so fast I trip over the ageless beach-bum mums in my haste to make it to the door.

In the midst of a reflection, hovering between subconsciousness and sleep, something strange has happened. I collapse in the driver's seat of my car outside the studio, not going anywhere. Rain thrashes the windscreen and I am awake, alive, present.

In my private corner in a dark room on a Tuesday at the bottom of the world, my dad has started speaking to me. Finally, I'm ready to listen.

TWENTY

INT. WAITING ROOM IN NETHER—AGAIN

An afterlife processing centre for suicides. It's stark, empty apart from RAYMOND SEIDLER and CHESTER BENNINGTON, who sit facing one another on opposite rows of faded orange stack chairs. Both have deep purple bruising around their necks. RAYMOND sits straight, as if keenly focusing on his posture. He is wearing bootcut jeans, R.M. Williams on his feet and a faded black leather jacket that reads 'Mission Impossible II: Crew'. CHESTER, legs akimbo, slouches back in his seat in what can only be described as rockstar touring attire: beanie, grey tank, skinny jeans. Tattoos snarl down his forearms and up from his chest, which RAYMOND regards with quiet disgust. Both sport reading glasses. They are bored, and angry at how bored they are.

RAYMOND

Explain it to me again.

CHESTER

I don't really see the point.

RAYMOND

That's not the point.

CHESTER

Man, if you're not open to what I'm saying . . .

RAYMOND

No. Yes. I am. I'm open. I need to understand. Tell me again.

CHESTER slides up in his chair, rubbing his neck. He is now eye level with RAYMOND.

CHESTER

Let's try it like this. Did you like your parents?

RAYMOND

Nobody likes their parents.

CHESTER

Hate them, then?

RAYMOND

Hate is a strong word.

CHESTER

So you did.

RAYMOND

Did what?

CHESTER

Hate them.

RAYMOND

Yes. My father mostly, but eventually her too.

CHESTER

He left?

RAYMOND

How did you—

CHESTER

We have twenty million fans. A lot of them write to us. Someone always leaves.

RAYMOND looks uncomfortable. He now starts scratching his neck.

RAYMOND

Christ, this burns.

CHESTER

If it didn't, it wouldn't have done the job . . . So?

RAYMOND

We were abandoned, in the snow. He wasn't well, but
that wasn't my fault. I was only thirteen. Thirteen and
man of the bloody house, how was I—

CHESTER

—Stop.

RAYMOND

What?

CHESTER

You feel that? Like your heart is going to explode there's
so much blood rushing into it?

RAYMOND

Chester, I'm dead. You're dead.

CHESTER

But you feel it, don't you.

RAYMOND

Yes.

They stare at each other. We get the impression RAYMOND
is truly seeing CHESTER for the first time. Without fanfare,
CHESTER gets up and moves over to RAYMOND's side
of the room so they are sitting side by side.

RAYMOND

What was the appeal?

CHESTER

I don't think our popularity came from our ambivalence.

RAYMOND

You felt it, you identified. A sort of tribe.

CHESTER

Not exactly a new concept. I was a punk. You would have been, what . . . a hippie?

RAYMOND

Disco, actually. Disco and jazz.

CHESTER

Well, that bucks the trend.

RAYMOND

He hated jazz, my father. His brother did, too. Used to come to our house in a fucking bowtie on a Sunday, make us play Bach.

CHESTER

I stand corrected.

RAYMOND

The world made fun of disco, but there was a lot of pain in it.

CHESTER

Michael Jackson definitely hated his dad.

RAYMOND

I don't think anyone will argue the point on that.

Both men stretch in their seats, which are horrendously uncomfortable. They are unsure if they want to continue with the conversation, but CHESTER decides to press on.

CHESTER

So, your father left.

RAYMOND

He had a younger lover. He must have been writing to her, it was the sixties. I woke up one morning and he'd booked himself onto a train and disappeared.

CHESTER

Did you miss him?

RAYMOND

Not at first. He was manic-depressive, but they hadn't invented that yet. The guy was a lot of work.

CHESTER

My dad was a cop. Worked on child sex abuse cases. Worked so hard that he didn't notice what my older friend was doing to me.

RAYMOND (WHISTLES)

Jeee-sus . . .

CHESTER

Gave up on him a long time ago.

RAYMOND gestures to the cavernously empty room.

RAYMOND

You may have made the right call on that one.

CHESTER laughs haltingly.

RAYMOND

Honestly? I'm a bit embarrassed.

CHESTER

You are?

RAYMOND

My life seems like a cakewalk compared to yours.

CHESTER

Everyone's pain is unique to them.

RAYMOND

You know, I used to say something similar to my son.

CHESTER

The one who joined our fan club on your credit card?

RAYMOND

[Basil Fawlty impersonation] Don't mention the war!

CHESTER

So, what was going on?

RAYMOND

He was depressed. Said he wanted to kill himself.

Silence. RAYMOND sighs, loudly.

RAYMOND

To think, we could have been in Nirvana instead of this dump.

CHESTER cranes his neck to look down the hall.

CHESTER

He should be around, actually.

RAYMOND

Who?

CHESTER

Kurt Cobain. Gunshot wound, though. Haven't seen many of them around.

RAYMOND

Ah, yes. 'Smells Like Teen Spirit'. Hated it. So abrasive, so . . .

CHESTER

Angry?

RAYMOND

I thought I could keep the kids away from it, but it just lit this fuse and the fire never went out.

CHESTER

And then we came along.

RAYMOND

When was that? 2000?

CHESTER

Sounds about right.

RAYMOND

He would have been thirteen.

CHESTER

Just like you were.

RAYMOND

Gelled his spikes so pointy for his bar mitzvah you could have snapped them clean off.

CHESTER

But you didn't leave.

RAYMOND

Yes, I did. I ran so many times.

CHESTER

Not like your father. You always came back.

CHESTER turns to RAYMOND as if to offer some form of comfort. But RAYMOND just hunches over and looks at the floor, refusing to catch his eye.

RAYMOND

You could have made something positive.

CHESTER

It was the end of the nineties.

RAYMOND

What's that got to do with the price of fish?

CHESTER

You've heard me sing. I wasn't going to be the next Bill Withers.

RAYMOND

Well, when you're not howling like a banshee, you actually have quite a nice voice.

CHESTER

That's the nicest thing anyone's said to me in this lifetime.

RAYMOND

I'm serious.

CHESTER

And I'm not?

Silence. Frustrated, CHESTER springs out of his chair, pacing about the room.

> CHESTER
>
> We sounded to you like jazz did to your uncle.

> RAYMOND
>
> I find that hard to believe.

> CHESTER
>
> No, you don't. You were born in the fifties? That's pretty much when the teenager was invented, man. You must've seen this happen four or five times by now.

> RAYMOND
>
> It was never this offensive. This aggressive.

CHESTER stares at RAYMOND incredulously.

> CHESTER
>
> Sid Vicious.

CHESTER starts ticking off his fingers.

> CHESTER
>
> Iggy Pop.

> RAYMOND
>
> Treated him once.

CHESTER

Ozzy Osbourne. Axl Rose. Keith Flint. *Chris Cornell.*

CHESTER pauses again and looks both ways, as if expecting Cornell to appear.

RAYMOND

Yes, alright. You've made your point.

CHESTER

I get it; we were really loud. That was by design. Ray, how many audio tracks do you think there are on a typical Top 40 rock song?

RAYMOND pauses to think.

RAYMOND

Ten?

CHESTER

About sixteen. Our first single, the one that your son loved? Eighty. Eighty tracks. Just try to comprehend that much sound. You can't. Your brain can't separate it all. So many layers of reverb, overdubs, effects. Left channel, right channel. Duplicates. Hi-hats replayed over crash cymbals. Bucketloads of screaming. Walls of guitars. Not Jimi's Marshall Stacks, I mean actual fucking *walls*. That's why we sounded louder. Because we were.

RAYMOND

How do you even do that?

CHESTER

If I told you I'd have to kill you.

They laugh.

RAYMOND

I've just realised something. My son hates me.

CHESTER

I wouldn't go that far, dude.

RAYMOND

Why not? All evidence points in that direction.

CHESTER

Hate is like love. Or fear. It's a hot emotion. It's very difficult to hold on to forever.

RAYMOND

The screaming philosopher.

CHESTER

My calendar is free for speaking engagements for the next eternity.

Raymond pauses.

RAYMOND

I hated him forever.

CHESTER

No, you didn't. You were thirteen. Nobody knows forgiveness at that age.

RAYMOND

I'm 61 now.

CHESTER

I'm 41. And we're both done.

RAYMOND

Done?

CHESTER

Done with the cycle. Carrying that weight around, passing it down the line, infecting everyone around us.

RAYMOND

I left. I left when he was thirteen years old and I kept leaving until I couldn't come back.

CHESTER

But he had something, right? Something you didn't.

RAYMOND

I bloody hope so.

FADE TO BLACK.

TWENTY-ONE

'I don't understand,' she said. 'Why wouldn't you want to have children with me?'

We were at an Ethiopian restaurant in Kreuzberg, on one of the final nights of a three-week trip we had started as near strangers. I was a few weeks off 30. Lena was nineteen. I had met her earlier that year in New Orleans on the serendipitous advice of my sister, who was sharing a room with her in college at the time. Now we were together in Berlin, continuing an international odyssey that mostly involved fucking around the clock and occasionally pausing to eat or look at art.

Lena was Swedish, and filled with the incredible self-confidence that comes with being effortlessly and beautifully Nordic. She spoke a great many more languages than I did.

All of her clothing choices were impeccable. I was obsessed with her.

'It's pretty simple,' I said. 'These things are often hereditary.'

'What has that got to do with anything?'

'It has everything to do with it.'

Aware of her magnetism, Lena backed herself. This meant she enjoyed deep, lingering eye contact. When she got mad, her crystal blue gaze crackled with violent electricity.

'So you say you love hanging out with me, you think I'm amazing and you want to be around me all the time, but you wouldn't have kids with me?'

'It's not about you,' I said, counting out grubby notes for the bill. 'It's about your genes.'

Zara had been understandably furious upon discovering I was sleeping with her roommate. 'I can't fucking believe you,' she fumed over Shabbat dinner a few months after the New Orleans incident. 'You couldn't have found anyone else? How many girls are there in the world, really?'

When she found out Lena and I had conspired long-range over text to meet in Amsterdam, despite knowing next to nothing about one another, she stopped talking to me entirely. But before, when we had been on better terms, she'd intimated that Lena wasn't 'all there'. She had a history of bulimia for which she had been hospitalised. In addition, her father was seriously mentally unwell. None of this was her fault, but I had been conditioned to see these sorts of things as red flags.

'Also,' Zara had added, grabbing another piece of sesame Challah as it sailed by her plate, 'She's one hundred per cent a narcissist.'

* * *

We stepped outside. I lit a menthol. Lena kept at it.

'That's not fair. Just because my dad is sick doesn't mean—'

'Stop it. You're still a student. Why are we even talking about this?'

'I want to know that you're devoted to me,' she said, with the sort of gravity that can only be non-ironic when you're up to your ears in critical theory.

'This is a pointless hypothetical. We're not dating. We're not married. In a few days you'll go back to Uppsala.'

'What if we did end up together? Would you still not want kids with me?'

By this point it was undeniable that I was a third-generation inheritor of wonky mental health. There was a clear line that ran through me and down to my hypothetical next of kin. I knew that any chance I was given to dilute that gene, the better. I don't care if you marry someone Jewish, Mum had always said half jokingly. Just marry someone normal.

'Lena, I've lived with this for years. It's not a joke. I'd never want to pass this on to my child. Imagine knowing that you could prevent them from having to feel all this pain. You've been depressed. What would you do?'

'You don't know that would happen,' she said quietly. 'You're just making excuses.'

'Your dad is sick. My dad is dead. We're both a bit crazy. Do you like those odds?'

* * *

Regular people don't fly halfway across the world on a whim that there might still be sexual chemistry with someone who they barely know and who is young enough to have never had to rewind a VHS tape. It occurred to me as we walked back down along the canal towards Paul-Lincke-Ufer, bickering with each other, that this entire vacation was likely a product of extended mania. I had barely been sleeping, and had no appetite apart from Lena herself. I was running on empty but somehow overflowing at the same time. When I heard stories from strangers drinking by the river, they felt like prophecies. The whole plot felt weirdly familiar, like a well-worn Raymond Carver story.

We paused at the traffic lights on Mariannenstraße and I stopped dead. This was a bad rerun of something I'd heard before: my own family history. The words tumbled out of me like I'd forgotten she was even there.

'When my grandfather was young, he was just totally off the wall. He'd sleep around on my grandmother and then go into these bouts of melancholy and nobody could get him out of bed. One day he picked up and left my dad, my aunt and grandma and caught a plane to meet this young lover he'd been secretly communicating with the whole time . . .'

'I don't understand, what are you saying?'

'I can't escape it, Lena. I'm just like him, on this intimate tour of Europe with someone I've met once while I was drunk. Does nothing about that strike you as strange? Really, I need to be more careful. There's just no way I would ever have kids with you.'

Earlier that day we'd taken the S-Bahn out to Teufelsberg, an abandoned spy tower in the middle of Grunewald Forest. We'd been in Berlin five nights and hadn't gone to one nightclub, too concerned with staying undressed to deal with the bouncers at Berghain. The tower had become a haven for the city's graffiti artists, who'd painted huge murals across every floor. On the penultimate landing, behind a tattered brown velour couch someone had hauled up all those stairs was a loud piece wedged full of cartoon lettering that simply read 'Fuck Fuck Fuck Fuck Fuck.' We took hundreds of photos in front of it, sometimes together, but mostly alone.

'You know what I think? You're so wrapped up in your little mental health myth you've forgotten how the real world works,' Lena snapped.

'Maybe you're right. But I still don't want to risk it.'

We stopped at the heavy gate to the apartment we technically weren't letting because Airbnb was still technically illegal in Berlin. I fumbled for the keys.

'We would make such good parents. You would be such a great father.'

'How can you seriously be thinking this way? You haven't even finished your degree,' I said.

'Don't make this about my age. That's a cheap argument. I know what I want.'

* * *

Years later, when Keren and I were trying for a baby, we went to the doctor for a check-up to make sure everything was in order.

'Alright,' he'd said, typing away. 'Any family history we need to know about?'

We thought about it.

'My dad had bowel cancer,' Keren said. 'But he's fully recovered.'

The doctor swivelled on his chair and turned to me. 'What about you?'

By 2020, we could genetically screen for over 300 rare disorders. The doctor had told us that a simple spit test sent off to America could tell us if our potential baby would have too many X chromosomes, or a rare genetic snafu where they died within a month, or had weak organs or brain deficiencies that would never have been picked up otherwise. It cost $750 and apparently it was a miracle of science. You couldn't change the genetic lottery, but you could certainly level your expectations.

There was no way to screen for any chronic mental health conditions. Testing could show us if a foetal brain wasn't developing, but couldn't yet peer inside it. We would be just as in the dark as Nana was about Dad, or he was about me. We'd hacked the future, but Keren and I were doomed to walk blindly towards the terrifying unknowns of the past.

I thought about this for a moment as I stared past the GP out the window.

'Nope, nothing on my side,' I said. 'Everyone is stupidly healthy.'

* * *

'I'm glad you know what you want,' I said to Lena. 'I mean that.' The gate to the building clicked behind us. 'Here's what I don't want. I don't want a child that falls behind in class because he can't get out of bed in the morning. I don't want a child that can't make friends, who has no self-belief, that we have to start medicating when they're still at school. I don't want a child that can't control himself, who feels too sad or anxious or down or up or all of those things and it takes over his life and becomes the thing that defines him. I don't want a child that has to get sectioned and end up a ward of the state. I don't want a child that thinks he wants to die because it's the only way out—or even worse: a child that decides to go through with it. I don't want to look up at that window up there where our room is, Lena, and see our kid standing at the edge about to jump. I would rather never have any kids—ever—than deal with that.'

Protracted, awkward silence. We stood in the open court-yard and I wondered how many other tenants had just overheard us fighting over figments. I thought about my birthday coming up, that I was turning 30 and was less in control of my emotions than ever. Lena grabbed my hand and slid it around her waist as we headed across to our building, past the stacks of rusted old bikes and little beds of roses peeking out over the concrete.

'It's fine babe, I'll drop it. Let's get back to bed.'

TWENTY-TWO

Nobody needs a bread maker, really. In the same way that most domestic kitchens have little use for a deep-fryer, milkshake maker, industrial slow cooker or grilled cheese jaffle press, the fancy machine is used a grand total of four times before joining the white plastic scrap heap that forms the inner bowels of our kitchen storage system. Dad buys these things for Mum at least once a year, and always at a time in which he should be investing in something thoughtful or romantic. They arrive in conspicuously wrapped oversized boxes on her birthday, Mother's Day, the eighth day of Hanukkah. Even Valentine's Day is not immune from whatever catalogue Dad's been reading on the toilet. 'Really,' Mum sighs on her forty-fifth birthday as she unveils a personal stone oven pizza maker. 'You're telling me the spa retreats were all sold out?'

In these pristine days of the proto-internet, nobody but social scientists and message board trolls even know what a meme is yet, let alone its future applications. But in our shambolic six-person house, these gifts are how it begins: it's a joke repeated so often that it sheds its skin and transcends its original context. It's funny without needing to explain itself, a signifier signifying nothing.

Dad's not entirely tone deaf and knows this style of largesse isn't considered top form from an oft-absent husband. He might not remember how his appliance romance started, but as an early advocate of web-surfing he just can't resist the meme—especially when he realises how much glee another cappuccino milk-frother will bring the rest of us. In a sense, this means each new contraption is a gift for the entire family excepting the person for whom it was intended, which is seemingly a clause in the unwritten contract one signs upon becoming a mother.

When Dad's illness digs in for real, one of the earliest casualties is his unrivalled capacity to wheel out jaw-droppingly useless presents. He starts buying Mum the things she actually wants, or hands over store-bought Hallmark numbers that function as IOUs. We're no longer at the age where we're barrelling into our parents' rooms to show off our precociousness with hand-made birthday cards written with our hard-won pen licences, but the lack of general cheer is palpable. Dad seems to hide inside himself, without his usual home appliance catalogue zeal, stopping only to ask us what we've bought for our mother and admonishing us if we haven't yet gotten around to it. One year Mum buys herself a Thermomix. It's a highly specialised German contraption that processes food at multiple temperature points simultaneously. You can make ice-cream in it and you can make soup in it. You can blend cold things and then simmer them. It's completely fucking ridiculous and it costs $1200. The worst part is that Dad isn't lugging it up the stairs for her, extolling its virtues while she dreams about far-off island holidays. Mum's had to flip the script and remix the meme to suit herself. The things that used to drive her mad are now what she misses the most.

* * *

You can grow approximately fuck-all in Central London, but it's easy to access those that can. London is a Mecca of imported food, bringing in all the best goods from its surrounding regions at competitive prices. I don't realise how much of Dad I've taken on until I find myself in a Turkish supermarket discussing the provenance of sucuk and chilli garlic olives while stocking a bag with Spanish cherry tomatoes and Iranian flatbread. It's all going towards the fresh breakfast I make every morning. If there's one thing Ray detested more than wowsers or anti-vaxxers, it was the idea of going out and paying for breakfast. 'Twelve bucks for avocado on toast? I could buy a bloody crate of them for that price! Why buy it when you could make it yourself?'

Dad loved the idea of becoming self-sufficient, creating stuff. Our kitchen was like a confused full-service restaurant. He baked bread, fried pizza, slow-cooked lamb. The man made preserves, rhubarb jam, marmalade, olives, pickles. He did yoghurt, tzatziki, falafel, wraps and his own hot chips. In the yard we grew tomatoes, oranges, lemons, rocket, mint, parsley and strawberries.

That's before you get to all his mates out at the markets. Ray refused to shop at Coles or Woolies. Straight to the source, he always said. Follow him out to Flemington at 6 a.m. and he's got his tomato guy and his Lebanese flatbread guy and they all know him. He's like a bloody celebrity, the private citizen hanging out at the wholesalers, talking shop. Came home with a box of mangoes he bought for five bucks, just beaming.

Sometimes I honestly reckon he would have been stoked to just move to the country and never blow money at a restaurant again in his life.

And so one cold February morning in Hackney I blink, and the past and present snap into focus. Like Dad, I have my apple guy at Broadway Market on Saturdays. He's Polish, and always holds the bag while it's on the scale so he can undercharge the regulars. Around the corner, the Kurds have the best hummus and vegetables plucked from fields all over Europe. Our groceries come from six destinations every week, just so I can manhandle the produce and talk to the purveyors. I am afforded this time as a freelancer, but I could just as easily have spent it all sinking pints. Something strange is compelling me to do this, to thrash my single speed around Dalston, backpack bursting with parsley, blackberries and a kilogram of de-bearded mussels.

I start to revise the story I always presumed to be true where Mum bought and made all the food while Dad went to work. Flashing back through VHS vignettes of history, I see entire weekends of Dad pottering about in the kitchen, always experimenting, cooking up something mad he suddenly decided was in his wheelhouse. 'Here, try this,' he says, scooping up some fresh peach compote or a spicy homemade laksa. There is rarely a Sunday where you can get to the fridge without having to also ingest some new creation Dad improvised from a picture he saw in the lifestyle section of yesterday's paper.

There's never a cookbook in shot. Somehow, despite growing up in a cold and bitter house still reeling from the shock of separation and divorce, where nearly every meal was beige or nuked, he's learned to cook by feel. And I want to reach out to him through the layers of reported truth that we call personal history and tell him how amazing that is. What an incredible legacy for a father to have passed down: of cooking, family and food. I finally appreciate it, now that

I've finally fallen in love properly and am making meals for my partner as often as I can. Our flat's fridge is more stocked than the one in her house ever was; even though she's also a fabulous cook, Keren works long London hours and doesn't have that same innate drive. 'Before I met you,' she says, spearing another slice of roasted miso eggplant, 'all I ate was packaged slices of M&S chicken for dinner.'

It really comes down to breakfast, though. At 32 and on the other side of the world, my breakfast has become a carbon copy of Ray's at 52. Eggs, flatbread, muesli, homemade espresso from a Bialetti. Like the cupboard full of appliances, some of which have survived the transition to a new house he'll never see, this spread has wrangled its way into a meme. It's a looping track without a starting point, one that I'll probably remix and redistribute to my own kids without remembering why I'm doing it. Every so often, when I'm really hungover, Keren convinces me to go out for breakfast at one of the myriad cafes on our road. I sit and chew, silently cursing the delicious dish that I probably could have made at home.

A few years after Dad dies, us kids toy with the idea of buying Mum a pointless kitchen appliance for her birthday. If we can just transplant the humour successfully from its practitioner, we may have a shot at reviving this strange slice of family joy. We don't explicitly say it, but we're aware this is one of those ephemeral memories that will be snuffed out if we don't work extra hard to keep it alive. It's not a beach holiday or a bar mitzvah. There are no direct references in any photo albums. It just has to become a Thing We Do.

The idea is summarily killed by Zara in the sibling group chat. 'No,' she types quickly. 'No fucking way. Are you out of your mind? Why would she want that?'

Maybe she's right—it'd never take. Mum gets a dressing gown for her sixtieth. All the spa retreats were sold out.

TWENTY-THREE

To understand Linkin Park, you really need to understand diamond sales. From the vantage point of the 2020s in which we now measure an artist's success in billions of streams that each equate to an infinitesimal fraction of a cent, the prospect of diamond sales seems remarkably antiquated. It brings to mind the heyday of multi-level CD stores with rows upon rows of gleaming jewel cases, shrink-wrapped and priced at $29.99 a pop, which isn't that long ago, really. Changes brought about by the internet have rewired every aspect of the entertainment industry, but none more so than music, which was blindsided first by Napster in the late nineties and has since had to evolve constantly to stay afloat. It says a lot that I can vividly remember using all my lawnmowing and car-washing savings to buy a new Beck album on CD, while I am now listening to that same album as I write this, for which I have paid the princely sum of $9 a month to access—along with practically every song in the history of recorded music.

Becoming a diamond-selling artist is an almost unfathomable concept. Imagine coping with the incredible stress that arrives when you discover that not only are you ridiculously popular, but suddenly you're the breadwinner for a team of hundreds of people and an economic concern for a gigantic licensing machine across the world. You could imagine it's something similar to being a father to many children, of which Chester had six: the demands just never stop. Linkin Park emerged at a time when men in rock music were compelled to succeed; they would be among the last bands to bother the top end of the charts for nearly a decade. Studio budgets were big, money was flying around everywhere, and label advances could be ludicrous. Failure was not an option; any vulnerability was best left in the lyrics. Linkin Park weren't in it to win it; fame clearly wasn't their motivation for writing music. But it came for them anyway.

Diamond sales mean different things in different territories, but the basic understanding is that it means you have obliterated the charts in a way that very few others have. Most countries take their cues from the Recording Industry Association of America (RIAA) Certification, which classifies sales benchmarks in Olympian terms, starting at the top and going up from there: Gold, Platinum and Diamond. As the general public, we typically hear mostly of gold and platinum sales, which correspond to 500,000 and a million album sales respectively in the US. For a scale comparison, the top-selling album in Australia of all time is John Farnham's *Whispering Jack,* which as of 2018 had sold 1.68 million copies. That's barely one platinum certification in the States, but down here, where you only need to shift 70,000 units to get one of those shiny plaques, it's gone close to 25 times platinum. The point of all this is that if you are an artist who has multi-platinum or multi-diamond certification, particularly in countries with large populations, chances are you've entered a rare echelon.

As a kid, I can remember the exact moment I fell out of love with maths. I was in Year Five and we'd started on fractions and decimals, which I just could not get my head around. I was dropped out of the top class and continued to plummet all the way through the rest of school—but what I lost in understanding equations I made up for in an obsession with mathematical terminology. The realisation that the words 'million' and 'billion' actually meant something, multiples of multiples, hundreds of thousands and thousands of millions, blew my tiny mind. I recall learning the origin of megacorporation Google's name: the term 'googol', which means 10 to the power of 100, a number most of us can't even comprehend. Or the Roman punishment of decimation, where every tenth soldier would be executed for the insubordinate actions of their group. I'm still yet to figure out how to file my own taxes or what a 15 per cent discount actually equates to each time, but my fascination with strange mathematical terms has never gone away.

Diamond sales in America mean you've sold 10,000,000 albums. Let that sink in. That's the entire population of Portugal. There are a lot of zeros in that number. Linkin Park's *Hybrid Theory* wasn't just the overall bestselling album in the US in the year 2001—essentially meaning around one in every 50 Americans owned a copy—but the world. This doesn't even account for the surge of music piracy that was in full effect by this point; the number of households infected with the Linkin Park virus could easily have been three or four times higher.

Imagine you are a gifted singer with no discernible future, drafted into a new band at late notice. You've had a horrific childhood, rife with abuse, which has seeped into your adult life, and when you get the call you're flipping patties at Burger King to help pay for a drug habit you've had since you were a teenager. You join the new group and click and you write some songs together, which the label decides they like enough to send off for mastering. One night in November you drift off to sleep and wake to the sound of tens of millions of people across the world handing over money for your record. With the notable exception of Adele, this is one of the last moments in history that something like this has happened—from this point on, everything gets blurred in a mix of downloads and streams and fudged bundling numbers cooked up by rap A&Rs, with the album becoming secondary to the t-shirt and sticker pack. These days there're thousands of different ways to fake it into the Top 40, or to sell albums that are designed as loss leaders for merchandise or ticket sales or streaming juggernauts. Diamond classification still exists, but it's the result of a bunch of equations, not pure sales.

One of my great regrets in life was not pushing harder for an opportunity to interview Bennington. Through time I had the chance to meet almost all of his contemporaries, but somehow he always eluded me. Of the many questions I'd have asked, the big one would have been whether this newfound responsibility as the guy who sold all the records scared him. I'd want to know how he managed or didn't, how hard it was to stay sober when it would have been the easiest way to black out a mountain of expectation. It's often been said that there was a startling disconnect between Chester's stage and off-stage demeanour, that he was unfailingly polite for a man known mostly for screaming himself hoarse. If I'd had the chance to sit in a stuffy hotel room with Chester, his label PR fluttering anxiously nearby, maybe I'd have had the courage to stare him dead in those dark-brown eyes and ask that if he had his time again, would he have given all those sales back?

* * *

When their debut was released, Linkin Park's impact on the year 2000 was unmatched. Their nearest competitor, our friends Limp Bizkit, ranked twenty-second in total album sales that same year. More than a decade later, the Bizkit would eventually go six times platinum; *Hybrid Theory* was already nudging diamond status after only twelve months. Teetering on the precipice of decline, the bloated recording industry in 2000 was worth nearly US$15 billion, and Linkin Park suddenly found themselves in the manager's box. When we look historically at nu-metal, music writers tend to lump angry bands with hip-hop and industrial influences into the same category, but Linkin Park weren't even in the same universe. They pulled this feat off multiple times over their career; their second album *Meteora* went platinum in just over a week, and they'd eventually have six records with multi-platinum certifications.

These sorts of numbers and the speed at which they were attained are what we'd up until then typically associated with pop stars or classic rock. Around the time Linkin Park roared in from the fringes, Max Martin–produced boy bands and girl wonders like Backstreet Boys and Britney Spears were setting sales records every other week. In the year 2000, the Backstreet Boys released *Black & Blue*, the fastest-selling album of all time at five million sales in its first week globally, while Spears' *Oops! . . . I Did it Again* became the fastest-selling album by a female artist since the charts began.

Meanwhile, The Eagles and Pink Floyd were still shifting millions of albums from generations ago, trying in vain to keep up with Michael Jackson's *Thriller*, still the bestselling album of all time.

It is impossible to understand Linkin Park without understanding the unbelievable pressure that being a diamond-selling rock band brings on to a group of young guys from diverse backgrounds who have never really had much money. In a 2020 ChartMasters wrap of the 50 top-selling albums ever, Linkin Park is one of only five acts released after the year 2000 to appear, alongside Eminem (twice), Adele and Norah Jones. As their alleged contemporaries fell away or out of favour, Linkin Park continued to write, record and release top-selling albums for close to twenty years. Like other multi-platinum, multi-year successes like AC/DC or Metallica, the fans of Linkin Park grew up, fell in love and had kids, all while continuing to listen to the band's music.

We tend to use celebrities as a mirror for our own anxieties—a way of creating shortcuts to discuss problems we may otherwise not be comfortable addressing. The throughlines associated with rock bands, particularly those comprised entirely of men, typically concern excess: drugs, money, violence, sex. These are the talking points that sell the magazines and papers I filed stories with for many years, and they leave little room for nuance. Few wanted to chat to Chester or Mike about more regular stuff, like self-doubt or feeling like they couldn't measure up as men, as fathers, when they were constantly on tour. There's nothing sexy about seeking happiness. I had enough teachers at school; those larger-than-life shirtless men stuck up on my bedroom wall were there because they took me away from the mundane. You couldn't achieve diamond sales by being content.

As is typically the way when a popular artist dies before their time, Chester Bennington's suicide in 2017 saw almost all of Linkin Park's records return to the charts. They've now sold in excess of 70 million albums worldwide, including those trillion invisible bits and bytes that we've since replaced our Discmans with. Seventy times platinum. Seven diamonds. It's something of a musical googol; you can say the number, but it's difficult to imagine what it really even means.

You know where I'm going with this. Sales are not every-thing. We all know critically acclaimed classics that have stood the test of time but never even shifted the needle when it came to recouping their label's investment. We know that Crazy Frog's 'Axel F' is the third-bestselling single of the twenty-first century in France. But we also know that big sales, hysterically large, internationally all-encompassing sales, are not an accident—that they meant something to the culture, and that they had a wide influence. From the invention of the teenager to the rise of the internet, society has continued to splinter into cults and niches that move ever further apart until someone like Beyoncé Knowles comes along. But here's the thing: at the time of Chester's death, Linkin Park had sold more records than Beyoncé. Like it or not, they are among our great musical unifiers.

You can walk into a bar or clothing store anywhere on Earth and hear them blasting out of the speakers. Staying that huge for that long is when being a rockstar stops being a novelty and becomes a responsibility. It's a lot to shoulder when you have a history of depression that's so well known it's become part of your group's DNA.

Sure, feel free to tell me that Linkin Park is juvenile, or aggressive, or that they were only big for one album, or only relevant for one moment when we all dyed our hair stupid colours and scribbled on our sneakers.

Throw whatever stones you've got.

When I see those diamonds, all I see is how much pressure went into making them.

TWENTY-FOUR

Dad disliked 85 per cent of my girlfriends, so I feel it's only fair that when I know I'm getting married I visit him and tell him. That I decide to do this at 5 a.m. on the morning of my wedding might seem like an afterthought, and that would be correct. But dead dads are not like living grandparents; they cannot guilt you from beyond the grave. Despite the fact that I haven't visited his plot in more than three years, I'm not anticipating the sort of sandpaper dry commentary I've come to expect from his mother, who I see about as frequently.

'Nice of you to come,' she says. 'I know you're very busy.'

'Of course not. I always have time for you.'

Nana is exceedingly well dressed for a Legitimately Old Person; she's always had such style. Even though she rarely leaves the house much these days, her outfits only get better.

Today she is wearing a head-to-toe monogrammed Burberry outfit in brown, gold and cream that would make Billie Eilish snarl with envy. One of her eyes glistens from recent surgery for macular degeneration, but as I don't see her that often I'm not 100 per cent sure which eye. Her apartment is full of furnishings that feel like they shouldn't be sat on or touched, all premium leather and angular glass tables. The maximum amount of time I have ever spent at Nana's house is two hours, and it was only this long because Dad was late to pick us up. In this respect it is the opposite of my maternal grandparents' house, which has housed us all for many sleepovers over the years.

My and Nana's relationship has been a bumpy ride. When I was fourteen and she was quarrelling with Dad—one of those epic 60-day freeze-outs where neither would talk to one another—I wrote her a letter telling her to fuck off and leave him alone, which I hand-delivered. A week later I received a reply in her spidery script. 'You may think whatever you like of me,' it read, 'but I am still your fucking grandmother.'

As Nana gets older and becomes increasingly isolated, I am trying to be the bigger person. I'm spending more time with her these days, and it turns out she's an absolute gas. For one, she has this way of commenting on my or any of her other grandsons' appearances that always borders on lascivious, especially when expressed through her unwaveringly thick Polish accent.

'You've grown *so* big. Or am I getting shorter?'

'Nana, you were always short.'

'That's not true. Maybe you were just a child then.'

'Twenty years ago? Sure,' I say.

'Anyway, it's nice of you to come. I thought you'd forgotten me.'

'Highly unlikely.'

'Look at this picture of your father. You look so much like him.'

After Dad died, his mother decided to build a shrine to him in her home. I can somewhat understand; Nana's European and over 90; this sort of self-immolation is just what people of her generation do. Nana once sat for Steven Spielberg to tell her story; she reminds me she still has it on tape. Trauma is never far away in her home.

There are more photos of my father in her house than ours.

* * *

The coronavirus has derailed our original plans for the wedding, but also made things significantly easier from an emotional standpoint, given a certain person's absence. I'm not going to be overwhelmed by guests because we're only allowed ten, with the rest dialling in from all over the world. The rabbi's going to be there, and my family, but pretty much nobody else. It feels like the whole world is disintegrating while we're getting married, which, given Judaism's penchant for mixing tragedy with celebration, seems entirely apt.

We're doing it in a close friend's backyard. Half the guests will be responsible for holding the chuppah in place that we hurriedly borrowed from the synagogue. Keren and I will be having our eight minutes in heaven—an actual requirement of orthodox Jewish marriages, not just a game for teenagers—in the blacked-out Kombi we've rented to drive her from the house, because our hosts won't let us inside.

But that's hours away yet. First, I need to figure out how to find Dad's grave. It's far too early to call anyone—and anyway I don't want to risk the embarrassment of admitting I have no idea where my own father is buried—so I take a punt and look up the cemetery website. As is tradition, my wife-to-be and I are required to spend the night before the wedding apart, so I'm in my mum's old room at Oma and Opa's house, which has not changed one iota since she lived there in the seventies. I'm sleeping on a rock-hard single bed surrounded by Presley paraphernalia, Chicago vinyl and black-and-white photos of Mum as a bronzed youth drinking Coca-Cola on the beach. I prop myself up on whatever passed for a pillow in the Nixon years and the blue glow from my phone blasts into my eyeballs as I tap Dad's name, date of birth and year of death into the 'Find a Loved One' search bar, expecting nothing.

* * *

Seidler, Raymond
Location: JEWISH MONUMENTAL, F27, GRAVE 0035
Co-ordinates: Longitude: 141.138576
Latitude: −38.787373

'Fuck me . . .' I gasp in the illuminated darkness. There's even a Google Maps link. I can drive my car along a straight blue line from this bed to Dad's final resting place and not even get remotely lost.

The gates open at 6 a.m. I get dressed before I have a chance to change my mind, and sneak out the front door, slipping on my Reeboks outside, careful not to wake Opa who is asleep in the back room. At the same moment, Oma is in hospital, livid that she's going to miss the biggest day of the third innings of her life because of a broken pelvis. But her rarely exercised rage hasn't stopped her consulting with the weather gods as she promised. Even at daybreak it's clear that this, the wedding day nobody had in their diaries until earlier this week, is going to be an absolute stunner.

Cranking Earth, Wind & Fire, I drive. In the new era of the modern plague, there's not a soul on the roads at the crack of dawn. I roll down the window on my now sixteen-year-old beaten-up Astra and let the air collide with my face.

I'm getting married today. I'm exhausted. This expedition is definitely not a bad decision made by someone who is delirious.

Maps has some difficulty with the internal paths of the cemetery, sprawling enough to constitute a London borough. It's a haphazardly planned city of the dead where the roads don't exactly connect; one wrong turn and you're in the Greek Orthodox section when you were looking for the Armenian lawn.

Maurice White is hitting the high notes of 'Boogie Wonderland' as I spin back around for the fourth time, looking for the elusive pin marking Dad's exact location. All around me gleam headstones adorned with crucifixes. I am totally, irrevocably lost and there is nobody here to ask for help.

* * *

We have far too many conversations about Dad's headstone— that's the sort of family we are. No standard set-up for the Seidlers, no—instead Mum decides to become a design director overnight, just at the point we are all starting to get back on with our lives.

I've returned to work at major creative agency Leo Burnett after a sizeable absence—and with a sizeable debt of gratitude for how nice they've been to me—when the request comes in from Mum for me to mock up a memorial design, despite the fact I am in no way an art director. Also, her brief has more copy on it than a bloated print ad.

For this hefty word count, the only choice left is a marble slab that lays on top of the grave instead of a simple marker indicating where it is. She's planning on a row of succulents and stones to run down the right-hand side of the slab, and along with everything else she needs our help crafting the text that will be chiselled into it.

Every few hours Mum is liaising with the guy, Mr Eisman, whose job it is to create such works of art, though it seems his primary talent is responding to complex inquiries with one-line answers.

It's fallen to me to put everything together because Eisman, despite designing graves, apparently is not actually a designer. He's got four or five templates, all of which are shit; he's used to just plugging in a Schwartz here and a Goldstein there. Nothing could have prepared him for the overwhelming extra-ness of my mother, nor her children, who after two weeks of intense and often blackly deadpan WhatsApping have finally settled on this absolute mouthful:

פ"נ יעקב בן משה
נפטר י"ח אב תשע"ג תנצב"ה

DR RAYMOND SEIDLER
March 6, 1952 – July 25, 2013

You will be deeply missed and
always loved by
your wife Debbie,
your children Jonathan, David,
Zac and Zara,
your mother, sister, in-laws and
extended family, as well as your
many friends and devoted patients.

Your mellifluous voice, smiling
eyes, quick wit,
sharp intellect, boundless curiosity
and compassion
will be with us forever, even if you
can't be

**We will love you every day
For the rest of our lives.**

At the agency, I have quickly learned that there is a time and place for extemporaneous prose, and in the case of communications, it's never. The golden rule of contemporary advertising is 'say more with less'; we are often referred to pieces from bygone years that feature barely any copy at all. Thus I find myself in a totally bullshit predicament: trying to find a designer at a place I've worked at barely three months who has an hour or two to help me reformat a gravestone that's about three paragraphs too long.

There's absolutely no way in hell I'm going to put someone random through this conversation, let alone try to explain why the family thinks it so important to etch the word 'mellifluous' into stone. I am mortified at the juiciness of our grief, the way it sloshes around in our collective bucket, threatening to spill over at any moment. This is nobody's problem but mine, so I quietly teach myself basic Photoshop and remake the thing from scratch, lest Eisman have to download a free font he's never heard of (it's Garamond) or lift more than one fat finger to make his five thousand bucks.

* * *

When I do find it, the headstone-cum-daybed ends up looking fucking great and remarkably original, which I'm allowed to say as I spend a very long time lost in a sea of upright markers that are all the damn same as each other. It's a crying shame there aren't any gravediggers out here, catching the early morning sun; there was something quite cinematic in my hooning around in an old Astra through this serene skatepark of the dead, trying to find someone who isn't actually there. In insisting Dad would have no traditional vertical marker, Mum believed she was creating a point of difference, setting her beloved apart from a veritable sea of Jacobsons and Woolfs. Instead, all she did was make him impossible to find.

I pull my third six-point turn of the day in the tiny, snaking rose-lined lane I eventually discover is called 'Shalom Way'. Beyond my filthy windscreen, a flock of birds soars out from a new-ish development of graves which I can just about recognise from repressed memory. Head down Main Avenue in this weird Americana small town of death and there he is, the hipster headless headstone in a crowd of mainstreamers.

'Cool.'

It's colder out here than I remember it was when I left the house less than an hour ago. Steam slaloms off my breath as the day drags itself awake, still not quite sure if it's deep autumn or the last days of summer. I'm parked less than ten steps from GRAVE 0035, but they feel like they might take all morning. The quiet is almost awesome. Cemeteries are never usually this still, with workers and grievers popping up on every corner. But here and now, time has stopped. I could shout at Dad and nobody would hear me.

My keys jingle as I make my way over, and as soon as I find what I've been looking for I perform an abrupt about-turn.

I've come all the way out here at the crack of dawn to stare in the other direction. For all my proselytising about men being able to open up and talk honestly, it turns out that in uncomfortable situations I still prefer silence.

But I came here to tell him, and since we don't believe in cremation I can't even pretend he's not down there. I turn back towards the onyx slab-stone, its endless waves of superfluous text glistening with dawn dew. But my eyes are drawn straight to the cavalcade of pictures of him from his families' shrines: handsome, young, bright and already irrevocably damaged. When Dad smiled it looked like he was a split second away from saying something side-splitting. He had the knowing grin of someone who had read the room before he'd even entered it. In sepia, in colour, in clippings, he was always the same. Charisma oozed out into the third dimension.

In these photos, there is absolutely no record of Dad's treatment-resistant depression, an equally dominant feature in his life. It's an invisible albatross passed down by his father, and quite possibly generations of fathers before that. If there was some sort of UV light for mood, you'd see the thing lingering in all of them; shadowing Dad into the room, nestling in the space between his shoulder and head, slowly wrapping itself around his neck. It's less a black dog than a soundless, scentless, slow aura, and under examination it's by far the most dominant feature.

There's nothing left to do. I am 32 years old on the verge of matrimony, so I stand at the last place I felt the weight of my father's body and talk to him about the woman who that afternoon will become my wife. If you've never had a close relation or friend die on you, it's unlikely you know the particularly strange catharsis of having a one-sided conversation with a spirit. There's absolutely no reason I couldn't have done this in my bedroom, or at the beach, or anywhere. We put Hebrew letters on the grave; someone among us believes in God. It also means we subscribe to the concept of the neshama, the soul and its agency after life. Dad isn't here; he is everywhere. He watches me as I sleep, as I write, as I fall in love. I don't have to tell him anything because he already knows it all.

We are a family of talkers; there is never a lot of oxygen to spare around our dinner table. Being interrupted is something we are all used to, so I speak slowly to Dad now, still unsure he isn't going to cut in with that mellifluous voice of his. Nothing comes, so I ramble on, telling him about Keren, how kind and warm she is, how much her father reminds me of him, and before I know it I'm into the real shit, eyes blurring, nose clogging as I berate him for not being there on my wedding day, leaving Mum there to walk me down the aisle alone. I ask him how I am supposed to be a good husband or a great father if I have nobody left to sound off against. My words don't echo; there's too much space and too many aslant surfaces here. They glance dully off endless rows of stone as I tell a forever 61-year-old father of four that I am terrified of being a sub-par father, of failing. That I don't want my child to suffer the way he and I have. I know this is a feeling he had often. I grasp at guidance that never comes.

Eventually I've got nothing left. I feel like I've puked all over this holy site; I'm bloodshot and hoarse. Still, nothing stirs. Something in me recommends I say Kaddish as a parting salvo, but I can't remember the words in their entirety and I'm not keen on looking any worse than I already do in front of the various spirits floating about.

I don't promise to visit soon, like I do with Nana. Instead, I just walk away, get in the car, and get lost four more times on my way out of the cemetery.

Mum got one part of the word salad on Dad's headstone right: he did have smiling eyes. If he'd ever broken the law, those eyes would have done him in; you'd be able to single them out of a line-up in a split second. Even when Dad was sad, the gaze remained the same. The smile behind his eyes might have been strained, or slightly muted, but it was still there. The only way he could get rid of it, this false hope so comically at odds with his chronic illness, was to get rid of himself. When his surviving mother and sister tell me I look exactly like my father, their son and brother, I know this is what they mean.

Later that day, a photographer takes close to 1000 shots of our brief but beautiful wedding. In every single photo, my eyes smile.

TWENTY-FIVE

It's getting dark on a Sunday afternoon as Dad sits down to write his book, the one he never wrote at all. The sun is melting beyond the back garden he's spent most of the day toiling over. A freshly cut lawn glistens through the hazy mist of sprinklers. In the two black bins under the frangipani tree, worms slowly turn apple cores and mango pits into fertiliser. It's a beautiful spring afternoon and everyone else has somewhere better to be, which suits Dad perfectly fine. He takes his milky tea and sugar biscuits and heads towards the study.

Dad needs absolute privacy when he writes because he doesn't actually write. Equally enamoured with new technology and the sound of his own voice, he is a firm proponent of Dragon Dictation, a sort of early-2000s Siri with three times the fail rate. Dad has been training his Dragon for about a year, slowly and methodically. It is his beloved fifth child, one that hangs on his every word and never talks back. He and his Dragon write letters to the *Sydney Morning Herald* and *Medical Observer*; they take patient notes and compile shopping lists for the markets. They compose blogs that no one but his mad patients and long-suffering family members read. The two are inseparable, and this afternoon they are embarking on their most top-secret project yet: the untold story of Ray's life.

He is paused mid-thought, something that doesn't parse well with his Dragon. The screen in front of him changes continuously, flicking between comma, line breaks and ellipses. Silence is the Achilles heel of voice-activated diction, but Dad can't figure out how to appropriately convey the idea that, much like the book he is not actually writing, he very nearly did not exist.

While he's frozen there, gaping stupidly at nothing, the way all creative people do when they're wrestling with an idea that seems both staggeringly brilliant and entirely insurmountable, it seems like a good place for me to step in. I'm the one who's going to end up telling it anyway.

* * *

We open on the exterior of a large passenger ship, docking in Sydney Harbour. It's the tail-end of the worst decade in human history and this boat is packed to the gunnels with destitute European refugees. They gaze upon the endless, sparkling blue water, wishing their families could see such splendour. One person desperate for a view on the overcrowded deck is Miriam, an attractive Polish girl barely out of her teens. Like most on board, the majority of Miriam's family has not survived the Holocaust. She has made this incredibly long journey to an unfamiliar country where she doesn't speak the language, has no money and only a few relatives. Miriam is part of the racial problem Australian delegates had previously announced to the Evian Conference that it was 'not desirous of importing'. She is lucky to have made it; many others have been turned away.

Unsure of their status in Australia—whether they are truly welcome or simply tolerated—European Jews like Miriam tend to cluster together. It is not unusual to attend a gathering of ex-refugees and hear Yiddish, German or Polish floating through the air. Sydney in the forties is the opposite of what most Ashkenazi Jews have ever experienced: loud, coarse, hot and rugged. There is an orchestra but no concert hall. Pubs close at six; most workers are sideways by five. Kugel and strolls on the Kärntner Straße have been replaced by an oppressive, tropical humidity for half the year and the insects to match. Sydney is somehow safe and wild at the same time. Everything is backwards and upside down.

Through montage, we watch as Miriam connects with others like her, attempting to fashion together the beginnings of some semblance of a life. A group of enterprising new arrivals who came out on one of the earlier boats has set about rustling up something of a social scene for those who have hurriedly relocated themselves Down Under. They organise plays and dances in the traditional style as a chance for single expats (which thanks to the war, almost everyone is) to meet each other. Young, naïve and beautiful, it doesn't take long for Miriam to quickly turn heads in her new community. She soon lands an invitation to one such society party, the hottest ticket in town, after catching the eye of a young Viennese transplant named Marcell Seidler. Somewhat serendipitously, she is only given the surname of her intended paramour. Miriam arrives looking dazzling and in search of this charming Mr Seidler; it certainly confuses matters when she is immediately swooped upon by Harry, Marcell's younger brother.

Harry is the Seidler who will become a household name in Australia. He is already a brilliant architect, and has arrived in Sydney at the behest of his mother, for whom he is building a futuristic spaceship disguised as a house that will shock the establishment. Harry is as close as one can get to a rockstar in the design world. Anyone even remotely related to him will be asked about this connection for the rest of their natural lives. Miriam, having unknowingly switched over the train tracks of fate, is immediately taken with this brash character. She dates Harry for months, only dimly aware that her original suitor, too well mannered to cut in and stake his original claim to her hand, remains waiting patiently in the wings.

In this alternate version, Marcell never gets the right words out. He unceremoniously exits this particular gene pool through no fault of his own, and soon after Miriam becomes Mrs Harry Seidler. She is increasingly drawn to the commanding young architect, already the talk of the town in his late twenties, and is fast-tracked to the good life. She attends university, teaches herself English and travels the world as the svelte partner of a brilliant and often brutal Modernist.

In the same vein, Harry also misses the function in which he was to meet the beguiling Penelope, daughter of esteemed barrister and state minister Clive Evatt QC. As Harry's profile continues to rise and the architectural awards rain down, all he sees is Miriam.

Nursing a broken heart but resigned to fate, Marcell is never far away. He and Miriam are in constant contact, especially after he is unofficially contracted to photograph all his brother's early buildings. Seeing the two of them over coffee one evening at the newly unveiled MLC Centre in central Sydney, we get the impression something more might be going on, but we never find out what it is.

Blessed with a disposable income for the first time in her life, Miriam starts purchasing the outfits she's been dreaming of since she arrived penniless in Sydney: eye-catching numbers in pastel pink and aquamarine, with perfectly paired jewellery. Marcell is there to keep her company, advising on cuts and cloth. He's also on hand when a local artist asks to paint Miriam's portrait, a large oil painting for a subject that fits the medium. It perfectly captures Miriam's gaze, soft and full despite a history of hardship, powerful enough to bore a hole in the opposing wall. In quieter moments, when his head isn't a flurry and dangerous ideas aren't keeping him up all night, Marcell considers asking Miriam if he can buy it.

Harry and Marcell are passionate people. They wear sharp suits and obsess over photography and art. A classic entrepreneur, Marcell will have many jobs over the years, but the longest standing will be shirt manufacturing. There is not a photo of either brother in which they don't appear immaculately turned out. The men love one another, even as they move apart professionally. While Harry is insanely driven, he is not mad—at least not in the same manner as his older brother, which is to say: irrevocably, clinically and resistant to treatment. Harry gets upset, to be sure. He often takes out full pages in the newspaper to blast the people of Sydney as backwards, culture-less ingrates, like when they rally against Jørn Utzon's radical vision for their new concert hall in Circular Quay. But he never takes himself to bed for months at a time. He never drains his savings on psychoanalysis, something Miriam likens to a Hollywood personal trainer, glamorous but totally useless. He is stable.

Nobody knows what the deal is with Miriam's brother-in-law. It could be post-war trauma, but then again, he was never really *in* it. His parents are alive; Rose has a famous house named for her. He and Harry were deported to an enemy alien camp in Canada when they were teenagers while most of their friends stayed around to watch their extended families die. The experience wasn't ideal, but it certainly could have been far worse. Marcell is devoted and doting, but it often feels more like obsession. Pull back and watch him sitting in the kitchen of his apartment, eating an entire punnet of cherries before lunch. Whole jars of pickles in one sitting. Nervous energy, legs always shaking beneath the glass table. Where is he putting it all? He can't weigh more than 75 kilos.

Marcell falls in and out of love with astonishing speed, takes up mistresses, even starts a sexual therapy business. He's interested in everything, but none of it is helping how he feels. Psychiatry is starting to become trendy, and while the Seidlers are ahead of the curve, nothing works on Marcell, not even shock treatment. He lies in bed for a month. Other times he doesn't sleep at all, writing furious memos that nobody will ever read, eyes bloodshot in the early hours of the morning.

Miriam thrives, Harry soars and Marcell unravels. His behaviour becomes more erratic; he starts disappearing for days, weeks at a time. Sometimes he talks so fast it seems like he has taken leave of his senses entirely. Other times he is as stubborn as a child, refusing to get out from under the covers, dead eyes sunk under the weight of his own doomed thoughts.

He is a brilliant man—'like a sponge', Miriam says—but he is hard work. Marcell has already cut professional ties with Harry, relinquishing the photography gig to Max Dupain. And Harry has already won two Sulman Medals; an Order of the British Empire and Order of Australia are not far off. Eventually, Miriam Seidler who is not Mrs Marcell Seidler but rather Mrs Harry Seidler, gives up. As her husband implores her, there is only so much she can do.

In this story, Marcell Seidler is not Miriam Seidler's problem, certainly not in the way he will become in her actual, real life. Unconsciously, she takes the path less travelled and neatly sidesteps her brother-in-law's implosion, which happens on both timelines. She is never messed around, she does not have to lie to her children—especially her eldest, Raymond— about where their philandering father is. She learns about abstract art and design instead of poring over dense psychology textbooks trying to teach herself how to fix her husband. Miriam has survived countless atrocities; the memory of the Holocaust is still fresh in her mind. Even in wealth and warmth she can still feel the bone cold chill of the Siberian gulag. Nobody expects her to have to deal with more heartbreak. There is a limit to how much one woman can take.

Towards the end of his short life, when he is still charming but no longer as dashing as he was when he first invited an attractive young Pole to his party, Marcell eventually decides to settle and marry the longest suffering of all his mistresses, a gossip writer at the *Sydney Morning Herald*. The wedding day arrives: a simple, pared-back reception in the increasingly exclusive hamlet of Point Piper. Miriam and the children are rehearsing their flower-throwing technique at the Chuppah down by the water. She is dressed splendidly for the occasion in a salmon taffeta dress Marcell picked out. It fits her compact frame like a glove. Miriam is happy for Marcell, who seems to have finally found someone who can tolerate his eccentricities, and she is looking forward to a less bumpy future with her brother-in-law. She stares out at the water, which she now lives above in a breathtaking apartment designed by her husband, and quietly marvels at the good fortune that has come her way after a history of very bad luck.

Half an hour later the string quartet has run out of entrance music but Marcell is still nowhere to be seen. His visibly distressed bride-to-be gestures wildly from her waiting position behind the hedge, but none of the guests knows where he is. Harry, in his finest tuxedo and worst mood, is dispatched to the Seidler apartment to shake some sense into Marcell. This is such typical behaviour, Harry fumes. Marcell is incapable of not blowing things up. Harry storms through the entry landing, hollering for his brother. Silence. He checks the kitchen, bathroom and bedrooms. He is losing patience quickly, the accent always rising in his words when his temper flares, and soon the walls vibrate with recriminations in German, the Seidlers' mother tongue.

Stück Scheiße . . .
Verdammter Scheiß . . .
Marcell! Hundesohn!

Harry is a stickler for details, but anger often obscures the obvious. It takes him a good ten minutes to realise the roller door is open, a pair of shiny black shoes neatly unlaced by the balcony ledge.

* * *

Dad stops, letting out a long sigh. His lips are chapped, tongue floppy from all the talking. It seemed like a great narrative device, this whole father switcheroo, but now he's worked himself into an ontological hole he'll unlikely be able to wriggle out of before he's summoned to get the barbecue fired up for dinner. The boys are getting so big that he's pretty much grilling an entire cow every night, worrying him from an environmental standpoint as much as an economic one. He's been trying to get the family to eat different types of food, with limited success. Of his four kids, only one will touch fish. They put tomato sauce on everything and fight over roast potatoes like prisoners. Soon they will grow up and eat all kinds of weird and wonderful crustaceans, but for now they are carnivorous little monsters. He stares at the screen, knowing he has to finish the story that never happened in the book that he'll ultimately never write or he won't be able to sleep tonight.

He clears his throat, noted by his Dragon as 'uh-Uh ahh'. He listens for the sound of shouting, doors slamming, computer speakers firing up. Anything that will give him an out, but no luck: the house is a tomb. Dad checks where the cursor is. He issues some pre-set 'delete' commands to get him back to square one. His Dragon is ready. There's nothing left to do.

* * *

In the early fifties, Miriam steps through one door that holds two possibilities, both of them ending in a Seidler man. But in this rendering of her life that Dad imagines, she does not become a direct casualty of severe mental illness. Marcell dies childless, his dark shadows stumbling off the third floor alongside him. I am never born. The ineffable sadness that often overtook Marcell, woozy blue nights stretching into whole seasons, will not similarly consume the lives of his descendants. The pain stops there. Marcell's death becomes a bandage to a flesh wound, bolstered by stitches and eventually replaced by new skin. Over time, Miriam and Harry's children and grandchildren will forget the cut was ever there.

She goes by Mara these days. Miriam was a bit too Jewish, Harry had said, and they didn't need to give anyone a reason to round them up again. Mara was far more cosmopolitan, he reasoned. It sounded like Paris and Stockholm. Glittering futures.

Now she is 93, and having survived both Seidler brothers Mara sits alone in her apartment, not far from where Marcell might have leapt off the face of the Earth. There are photos of her extended kin, but no memorials. Mara does not think back on the difficult, sparkling man she loved, the invincible night prowler who woke her from her sleep before slowly losing his mind. She does not spend her days chewing on the blandness of prolonged grief, thinking about her son who took his own life. Instead she watches the news, tends to her plants and sits on that same balcony each afternoon, watching the ships pull into Sydney Harbour, wondering at the unpredictability of human life.

Her downstairs neighbour turns 100 tomorrow. As always, Mara is invited to the party. Enough plutzing: it's time for her to get dressed.

* * *

'Full stop.'

'New paragraph.'

'Save and quit.'

TWENTY-SIX

When I was still a boy, not yet a man, our synagogue burned down. It was a mystery never fully solved; in a tale that convinced nobody, it was put down to faulty electrics. The fire burned all night, and by morning the house of worship was a charred exoskeleton. A sensational event by anyone's standards, for years afterward the Central Synagogue inferno remained shrouded in the sort of gothic undertones I'd soon realise hung around every Jewish tragedy. The twin ghouls of anti-Semitism and terrorism inserted themselves into stories that did not require them, like the one about the shul with dodgy wiring that grew from a flicker to a blaze before anyone could stop it.

The board and senior machers of the synagogue, all of whom were men, got to work immediately on a replacement. As is often the case when misfortune befalls an ethnic minority, a like-for-like was not even on the table. The new

Central would be a glow-up so significant that it would seem to the regular observer like the corner shop had gone up in flames and when the smoke cleared in its place was a Westfield. Brilliance was the only acceptable outcome.

The year following the fire, 1995, already augured disaster. Israeli Prime Minister Yitzhak Rabin had been assassinated by an unhinged fellow Jew, the writing was on the wall for the Oslo Peace Accords, and America's first real taste of homegrown terrorism, the Oklahoma City bombing, were just around the corner. Overnight, armed security guards appeared at the gates of my school—unheard of in Australia at the time—and never left. At age eight I participated in my first campus-wide bomb drill. Violent threats were phoned into our campus reception with increasing regularity. I was told by my teachers not to wear my kippah on the bus so as to avoid suspicion or reprisal from kids from other schools. Though unrelated, the fire seemed intrinsically wrapped up in the tenor of the times. Australia was at the end of the Earth, but fear had arrived.

The new temple took four years to build, a marvel of modern architecture and paranoia. Its large glass doors were able to withstand both gunfire and explosives. Bollards hidden beneath the footpath would total any car attempting to ram through the front entrance. There were multiple covert exits, endless marble floors and a central atrium that filtered in natural sunlight. In many ways it felt more like a sophisticated concert hall or luxury store than a house of worship. But in spite of its plush seats and purple carpeted floors, the shul was uncomfortable. It smelled like money. The overwhelming sensation you would receive as a young congregant was of being out of step with your station. It was likely not an accident that this retail iteration of religion would be erected a few hundred metres from the eventual site of one of the largest suburban malls in the Southern Hemisphere, both projects overseen by the same Auschwitz survivor who famously turned a single delivery van into a shopping empire.

People tended to talk about Central in terms of capacity, rather than congregation, as if it was some sort of exclusive opera venue. This made sense when you consider it seated more people than many of the concert halls in Sydney. Like those establishments, Central was obviously not designed for children. The doors were large and heavy, the floors were cold and unforgiving, and there were sharp edges everywhere. It was like that one room in our house we were never allowed to be in unless there were guests, a place I had decided I hated years before I ascended the Bimah with my unbroken voice and too-big prayer shawl that Dad kept having to re-drape over my tiny shoulders so I could become a man.

* * *

On the Friday night of my bar mitzvah, an intruder somehow breached security. The entire synagogue was locked down with my whole family inside. Concerned men with beige camo shirts and walkie-talkies fanned out across the atrium. I sat in the front row especially allocated for my special day, hair forcefully flattened and parted by Mum, whispering to my brothers, wondering if we were all about to be mowed down by an Uzi. Dying in a bloody massacre less than twelve hours before reaching the zenith of manhood would definitely make me the coolest kid in school, probably forever, I reasoned. Rachel, who right now wouldn't even look in my direction, would likely mourn me as long as she lived. Maybe one day she'd end up getting a tattoo of my name somewhere small beneath her ribs.

I looked to Dad for some solace, but he seemed largely concerned with the delayed onset of Friday night dinner, having likely skipped lunch to see extra patients. Dad's uniquely curated line of work meant he'd had a lot of experience with every brand of lunatic. No GP in Kings Cross was likely to steer clear of drama, but Ray seemed to actively invite it. Junkies pulled knives on him in his office, small-time crooks tried to swindle him out of scripts for pseudoephedrine they could use to cook up ecstasy, and Lebanese gangster bosses sent henchmen to get pills for their mothers out in the suburbs. I had never seen a gun in real life, but I bet Dad had. All the things that made him weird and esoteric, so frustratingly different from my friends' fathers, would probably be what would save us in a crisis situation. If push came to shove and the balaclava-clad

Uzi men blasted their way into the atrium, Ray would talk them down. He could level with anyone. Everyone liked him.

Dad's relationship to the synagogue was complicated. Despite having been married there, he seemed to actively despise what it stood for. Nonetheless, he firmly demanded our attendance. Often estranged from the living members of his own family, he used Central as a way of binding the men in his brood together. From the safe vantage of the cheap seats, hemmed in by my uncle and grandfather, the four of us could decry the specious money politics of the place together, make fun of the rabbi for being out of touch ('I read about this band the other day, called The Beatles . . .'), crack highly inappropriate jokes, open our machzors to the wrong page, or pledge $2000 in the high holiday appeal on behalf of the guy in the seat next to me who hadn't shown up. Occasionally Dad would snap at us, but that was mostly for show. Religion was less important for what it stood for than for what it achieved as a form of filial glue. As I got older I challenged Dad a few times on why synagogue was even necessary when none of us liked it, but by the time I thought about asking him if he believed in God, he'd already died.

* * *

It's a real shame Dad hadn't stopped by a Hungry Jack's as he headed to synagogue tonight—clear heads are always better for taking out terrorists.

Hot chips were his saviour. Sometimes when he was at a loose end after a particularly hectic day at the surgery, Dad snuck into the Darlinghurst Hungry Jack's for hot chips. Having spent a lifetime evangelising healthy eating, he'd never let me see it, but I could tell when he'd been at the fries. So could Mum, who would publicly admonish him for loading up on fast food before dinner. 'No potatoes for your father,' she'd announce sternly at the table, 'he's had plenty already.' What we all failed to realise was that Dad wasn't getting deep-fried goods purely to quell his hunger; here was a man who didn't believe in use-by dates, who slurped chicken skin, swallowed pips, devoured fish eyes and sheep brains. Rather, the chips represented a private, holy moment for Dad, sitting in his quietly purring Holden Calais two minutes from home, licking the salt off his fingers and fishing for the last fry in the bottom of the packet.

S i l e n c e.

It was here that he could commune with himself, or a higher power, or both. The face on Dad after he'd scoffed a large serve of chips was one of sublime divination. He meditated, practised breathing exercises, lit candles and listened to sixteen-minute versions of Pachelbel's 'Canon' performed over the sound of softly crashing waves, but nothing brought him close to the essence of oneness he attained by retaining sole control of his destiny for those few, greasy moments.

Dad especially liked to eat chips on the way to synagogue. Experiencing personal Zen from a non-kosher quick-service restaurant before arriving somewhere that austere was a kind of double orgasm. He'd close his eyes during service and fully disappear.

The Jewish private militia continued to pace back and forth, whispering code into their receivers and occasionally leaving the darkening inner sanctum to check on something unknown outside. There was nothing but the muted murmuring of my pre–bar mitzvah attendees, who by now definitely hated me, gazing around the giant space and waiting for a late round appearance from Elijah the Prophet—or even the Messiah himself, someone I'd always imagined to look a bit like Jeff Bridges.

After an interminable amount of time the coast was declared clear. The extended party was hustled out a secret back door with no explanation offered or requested. For all we knew there was some unfortunate swarthy guy riddled with bullets back by the toilets or a nihilistic McVeigh type in a headlock by reception with his errant backpack blown up around the corner as a precaution. Like most things to do with Central Synagogue, the events that had transpired the night before I was to become a man were above my pay grade.

* * *

Things changed when I eventually turned thirteen. For one, fasting on Yom Kippur, the most sacred day of the year, was now mandatory. I also wasn't allowed to show up late or shirk synagogue to go see *Star Wars* on the high holy days, instead being wedged in between Dad and Opa, totally brain-dead from boredom. Being a man meant responsibilities; in this case, staring blankly at reams of Ancient Hebrew and singing words I knew by rote but didn't understand at all.

Mercifully, other kids from school were also dragged to Central. We traded war stories together, hiding beneath the internal stairs leading to the hallowed women's section during The Break when our elders were obligated to stay inside. We took turns boasting about how hungry we were or how easy the fast was, and fantasised about the truckloads of junk food we were going to cram into our gullets the second this twisted ritual was done for another year. We were all dressed in the sort of mish-mash formalwear combos that represented the waning influence of our parents: Oxford shirts paired with baggy cords, suit pants with skate shoes, short-sleeved Hawaiian shirts over white crewnecks. We were a bunch of nerds trying to be street, mummy's boys trying to pass off as cool kids, every outfit modification an unspoken nod to the tantrums we'd thrown only a few hours prior.

'No, *no way* I'm not wearing that. It's not smart Mum, it's *dumb*. Why do you always have to make me look like such a fucking *dork*!?'

The girls we used to jostle with on the slide and trade recess snacks with now wore braces and bras. They towered over me no matter how high I walked on my tiptoes or how much product I scrunched through my hair. As per Orthodox tradition, they sat up in the heavens of the mezzanine level, far removed from me like the lanky goddesses they were.

We knew they also had to leave during The Break; this stairwell location was not chosen by accident. All around me hummed the chaos of boys-to-men steeling themselves for an influx of double X chromosomes. Danny assessed the state of his locks in the reflection of the swinging glass door. Gavin sat on the first step, obsessively breathing into his palm to check for bad breath. Josh practised his openers. The Break wasn't a stipulated length of time, but it was always too bloody short. There were very few chances to talk to the girls outside of the classroom or playground in the complete absence of authority. Without ever acknowledging it, we all knew these precious ten or fifteen minutes were where we truly made our mark as men.

My position was made more tenuous by the inescapable fact that Danny and I had eyes on the same woman. I'd been obsessed with Rachel all year, spending much of my allotted synagogue time daydreaming about holding her hand or pushing away those chestnut bangs, looking into her eyes and telling her with complete sincerity that I loved her. As a newly minted teenager, this textbook tragic approach is what I presumed would work wonders on the opposite sex, informed by a tidal wave of nineties movies in which I often rooted for the losing team. The saccharine songs that came attached to era-defining flicks like *She's All That, 10 Things I Hate About You* and *Romeo + Juliet* seemed bespoke to my situation. Among my burgeoning collection of aggressive rock music I began to covertly file soundtrack fillers like Sixpence None the Richer's 'Kiss Me', Gabrielle's 'Dreams' and far too many Des'ree ballads. This condition, it seemed to me, was earnestly terminal.

Danny, meanwhile, was the star of the basketball team. He had cool hair, actual shoulders and biceps and had already open-mouth-kissed girls at parties I hadn't been invited to. All I had to show for myself was a bunch of rhyming couplets I'd written about Rachel in the back of my exercise book and a rumbling stomach. Bringing my A-game charisma when my body was screaming out for sustenance was a daunting task. My parents had let me do a trial run of fasting the previous year, but I'd caved by lunch time. There were still seven hours left of this torture festival. Romance was very low on my hierarchy of needs.

A loud rumble overhead signified that the girls would soon be streaming out of synagogue. I scurried into position, eyes scanning rows of women as they filed noisily down the stairs and past Gavin who, in his panic, had forgotten to stand up. Alisa, Julia, Leah, two Sarahs and three Jessicas, all wearing spaghetti straps and skirts that likely provoked similar spats with their parents we'd had with ours. There was a rush of Lip Smackers and hair mousse, the disorienting glint of metallic braces. I held firm as the crowd emptied out, but Rachel was nowhere to be seen.

* * *

For the elders, The Break had a purpose. It was a prayer called Yizkor, which initially meant nothing to me other than a sign I'd be able to escape all the stinky old men and the sermons and the taped-together Torah I still had PTSD from having to read in front of everyone only a few months earlier. To me, Yizkor was the unofficial starter gun for fresh air and natural light, and as soon as I saw it coming up in the day's running order I was already making eyes at Josh like the 'let's make like a Tom and Cruise' joke I still found hilarious, packing my Jewish accoutrements quickly into a velvet bag and shoving it into my little seat locker, sliding past Dad, stepping over Opa's gangly legs, high-fiving my uncle and piss-bolting out the door before I heard a single word the rabbi said.

Soon the foyer would be stuffed with youth, including the older brothers and cousins, those twenty- and thirty-year-olds with little kids of their own. I figured Yizkor was the sort of thing we had to do when we got old, like the fact that we didn't have to fast before but now we did. Under the watchful eyes of security the mass soon thronged out into the street, desperate for the sunshine that always seemed to be in surplus on the day our people were condemned to be indoors. Too short to properly survey the crowd, I eventually spotted Danny playing handball with some of the other guys and figured maybe Rachel hadn't come to Central at all. The sun was blisteringly intense for September, and as I touched my head I could feel those perfectly aligned spikes I worked on all morning collapsing in the heat, along with puddles of sweat pooling in my jeans. She wasn't there. It was all for nothing. There was an unspoken ripple in the sea of congregants that indicated it was time to head back inside. I was so thirsty. Everything looked like food. Being a man was the pits.

* * *

Walking home later that afternoon I kicked aimlessly at tufts of grass and bits of asphalt, hanging back from the family. It was one of those double jeopardy years when Yom Kippur fell on a Saturday. Not only did we lose a whole golden weekend, but we were also blessed to feel the eyes of all the weekend drivers burning holes in our backs as they pulled up at red lights to let us cross the road. Acutely self-aware, I didn't have to know any of these people to be ashamed of being so overdressed. Up ahead, I could hear Mum quizzing David about my bad mood.

'He's just pissed off because Rachel didn't show up today.'

'Rachel?'

'You know, cousin of what's-her-name. The brother is in Zac's year. Pretty one, sings sometimes in assembly,' he said.

'Oh yes, the Schwartz girl. He likes her?'

'Mum, are you serious? He writes full-on fucking songs about her.'

'Piss off, David.' By now I'd caught up to them at a crossing. 'I don't like her, she just said she was going to bring me a CD.'

'Well, I hate to be the bearer of bad news, but she was there,' said Mum, casually ignoring the swearing that was clearly causing other congregants to turn their heads, tutting under their foul breaths.

'What do you mean? She clearly wasn't.'

'It's true, Jon was literally looking everywhere for her during The Break.'

'David, I swear I'm going to fucking—'

'Enough!' Mum snapped. 'Both of you, mind the language. And Jonathan, for your information, she was there today. Her family sits near us and I know her auntie. I remember because when we started leaving for Yizkor she didn't move from her seat. Poor girl . . .'

I grabbed my mother's arm a bit too forcefully. This was not part of the script. 'Impossible,' I said. 'Kids aren't supposed to stay for Yizkor.'

This damn traffic light was taking forever to change. Everyone was watching me.

'Exactly,' she sighed.

* * *

Yizkor is a prayer for the dead. It's the holiest moment during the most sanctified few days of the Jewish calendar, in which some believe the souls of the departed re-enter synagogue to be with their loved ones. Rabbis spend much of the high holy days begging for quiet, but only for Yizkor is it strictly enforced. Spirits tread lightly on air; noise can disturb the frequencies on which they travel. Being inside a synagogue during Yizkor is like being in a decompression chamber, an airless, vacuum-sealed tomb. Prayers are said, but mostly muttered. Moments of silence in society are not unique to Yizkor, of course. We honour our fallen, whether military or innocents, with similar gestures. The nature of Yizkor's silence, however, is different. It is intricate and perfectly buffed glass, beautiful but almost imperceptible. For ten minutes, one day a year, we are encased in Swarovski. Even the slightest tremor can shatter the structure.

As I progressed from a nominal adult into an actual one, I realised that to be allowed out into the sunshine for this brief window was to count your blessings. Yizkor was reserved for those whose immediate relatives had passed away. To be outside meant that nobody close to you had died: parents, siblings or children. It was generally accepted that no one would even be considering Yizkor until they were old enough to have their prostate checked.

Rachel hadn't told anyone at school that her mother had inoperable cancer. No one knew that when Roslyn came to watch her daughter sing at the talent contest she'd been wearing a sheitel to hide her bald head, summoning all her energy to put that sparkle back into her eyes, to whoop and cheer for her daughter. While I was writing terrible love songs about her only child, Rachel's mother had been finalising her affairs. The cancer had metastasised and run rampant through her bones. The oncologists had thrown the entire kitchen sink at it, but nothing stuck. She was barely 50 years old. Her private service had taken place during the holidays, and by the time the new term had started Rachel was sitting next to me in history class like nothing had ever happened.

That I'd missed this huge piece of information was stunning. I thought I knew everything about Rachel—and more to the point, I'd had a morbid fascination with Yizkor from even before my bar mitzvah. On the way out during The Break I'd often pause to look through the interior windows, where you could just about make out the mostly vacated women's rows, to try and get a sense of what this thing was all about. I wanted to know whether the ritual was subdued or animated, if the choir was in full force or the ark was open. It was intriguing to know what it felt like to be in there without actually having to share in the sombreness myself.

Peering into the atrium, I would gape at what felt like a weird TV show with the sound turned down. The remaining congregants seemed engaged in some sort of elegiac incantation. They were standing up but barely moving, separated by chunks of empty seats still warm from the presence of children and young men. Without being able to see much of the women's section, which was beyond the range of my secret porthole, the room seemed to vibrate softly with the intense sadness of slightly greying middle-aged men. Men who had lost key members of their families right as they were growing their own. Men who had buried wives and mothers. Men who had had to shovel dirt onto the bodies of their own sons. As I squinted through curved palms I could almost discern the faint outlines of the dead as they hovered in the spaces we had left, resting their cartoon palms on the shoulders of their bereaved earthly relatives.

* * *

None of this snooping adequately prepared me for the day I became a person who didn't go outside during The Break. I was told, naturally, that the first Yom Kippur without my father would be difficult, like his birthday or wedding anniversary. Not being a particularly religious person myself, I'd imagined it would be something of a formality. Recite a prayer, hear the choir, bow your head, enjoy the serenity. There surely had to be a disconnect between the awe I felt as an outside observer of Yizkor and the expectation of actually being a participant. The black suit I wore to his funeral still fit snugly, so at the very least I wouldn't look like an idiot. I was old enough to not find synagogue imposing anymore, even if I wasn't yet confident in my ability to defuse potential terrorist threats.

As with the passage of life, Yizkor exists on a continuum whereby honouring the dead is part of a constant chain of movement. There would be no induction for new recruits, even those like me who were very young, finding ourselves abandoned inside synagogue for the first time. Nothing could be quite as surreal as watching close to a thousand men file out the doors while staying rooted to one spot, as if the house lights had come on at the end of a Prince concert even though I was convinced he was going to come back and do 'Purple Rain' one more time just for me. Being an immovable object against a fast-moving stream meant I was sure to attract extra attention. Every man who walked past me, members of my community who had known me since I was born, tried to keep their eyes to the ground. It wasn't that they weren't sympathetic, it was just that they, like me, were still yet to fully grasp what my staying put for The Break really meant. Seeing me and my fatherless brothers in the back left bronze rows of the men's level likely conjured up ugly hypotheticals around their own mortality that they were not keen on entertaining. A few family friends made sad eyes in my direction, but nobody tried to hug or touch me. With a final click of the big swishing door, the lucky ones were gone.

There's not much to Yizkor, really. A few remarks from the rabbi, an anecdote about Israel or the Holocaust or some obscure new piece he found digging around the internet, and then the big finale, largely consisting of self-reflection and prayer. It is this part that I'd often watched from the other side of the glass as a teenager, observing a stillness that bordered on transcendental. Finding myself suddenly thrown into the hot seat, flanked by my much taller brothers, my uncle and my fast-shrinking grandfather, looking blankly at a bracha that offered a fill-in-the-blanks for someone who had died:

'Insert Hebrew Name _____, Father/Mother/Sister/ Brother/Son/Daughter of _____ who has gone on to the next world.'

I wondered if our being here was even appropriate. Transliteration aside, these short passages were patently designed for those who had died, rather than those who had chosen to die. The language was very clear. There was talk of being bound up with other righteous souls in the Garden of Eden, the Abrahams and Isaacs of our historical lineage, but that wasn't where I presumed Dad was hanging out. He surely wouldn't be able to spin a good yarn while tending the hedges with the people who always kept kosher.

Finding linguistic and logical flaws in prayers had been a favourite pastime each year I was herded into synagogue by my parents. Us three boys had revelled in dissecting the inane Talmudic explanations the way others made a life critiquing Shakespeare.

I broke from the meta-analysis and looked over to Zac to try to keep this cheekiness alive, but he was sobbing, gripping the bench in front of him like he might fall over. Beyond him, Opa, who I had never seen display any emotion aside from extreme love or irritation at losing a tennis match, seemed to have totally collapsed into himself. David stared straight ahead, blinking furiously. I was standing surrounded by family entering private worlds of sorrow, and this was not how I wanted to do it. The strategies I had for coping with this situation involved practically anything but airless, stale solemnity. Glimmers of ghosts I'd seen in the past were not at all forthcoming as I gently rocked back and forth on the balls of my feet, trying to magic myself to anywhere but this room. I wondered how Rachel had managed that first time she had to do Yizkor at only twelve, no sisters to surround or smother her into their chests when she broke down, murmuring shitty ancient prose that was somehow meant to comfort her.

In the dying minutes of self-reflection, as the shield I'd been labouring to hold upright for months finally started to break apart, I realised this was what Yizkor really was all about. Sitting with it. Staring at it. Dealing with it. Space and quiet to be with it. I had moved so fast through the past few months that by the time I had considered managing my trauma every aspect of it was already in the rear-view mirror. Yizkor was the loop round the suburban cul-de-sac that Dad had taught me to cycle as a child, where I skidded the brakes and ended right where I started. It was the moment Ray materialised out of nowhere, just where I'd left him, grabbing me in his hairy bear arms for an embrace and congratulating me on learning to finally ride on my own.

In Yizkor, two minutes can easily become two years. It's intense enough that once you accept it, you can drown yourself in it. The name is taken from the Hebrew root zachor, 'to remember'. Lock someone in your memories, tend to them each year to keep them fresh, and they're never truly gone.

* * *

The afternoon when I finally completed the bike loop, Dad had come prepared. He knelt down beside my blue BMX, jeans scraping the pavement as he jiggled around with the screwdriver. Without warning, one set of training wheels slipped off, then the other. I looked at him incredulously. Surely more practice was needed. I was totally unprepared for this.

'Listen, Jonathan,' he said. 'You're never ready for something until it whacks you in the arse.'

TWENTY-SEVEN

It's been two months since Keren lost the baby and every day it feels like one of us wants to throw up, but there's nothing left. The velocity with which the child went from being real to becoming a negative space is nauseating. Keren has only now just finished a battery of blood tests to ensure that the baby we were attempting to bring into the world has been fully flushed out of her body and won't inadvertently kill her. An ectopic pregnancy is the platinum edition of a miscarriage, with an avalanche of unknowns, constant monitoring, residual after effects and complementary late-night stays at the hospital. There is a mandatory two-cycle abstinence period before we are even allowed to try to conceive again. This is the purgatory we find ourselves in when someone uploads the video of one of David's school friend's gender reveal to the family chat.

It is not low-key. In fact, the entire display feels like some bizarre reality TV experiment. The clip opens on the dad-to-be shooting hoops at a park close to us. He's almost 30, but still has the frame of a gangly teenager who hasn't figured out where his limbs should go. To his left, a prearranged gaggle of family and friends watch on anxiously. Future father dribbles, considering a three pointer but instead—as he was always going to—rolls through for the lay-up. As he dramatically slams the ball against the backboard it triggers a hidden canister. Blue smoke pours out, filling the screen. It's a boy! What a scene!

Everyone in the frame starts cheering. Impending dad hugs his wife. The angle shifts and we realise that every element of this content has been scripted and that it's being filmed via drone. It's possible that this is not only an edit, but also the third or twenty-fifth take of the same set-up. It's the kind of stupid, overblown thing that would be completely hilarious if we were at any other point in our lives. Instead, it makes Keren profoundly angry. She goes into immediate shutdown, binges box sets in her dressing gown in the middle of the day, refusing to talk, eat or shower. We have been through this enough in the last little while to know that her statute of limitations is twelve hours, and that by tomorrow it'll be like nothing ever happened. For now, though, I have to get out of the way, so I put on my headphones, crank up some appropriately morose music like Laura Marling or Elliott

Smith, and roam the streets like I'm homeless. When I make it to the northern end of the beach, where the cliffs curl vertiginously over a vista of foam and tides smash against rocks, I sit on an empty bench in the fierce wind and type a poem into my phone that fixes nothing:

they leave it in
case they need
to dredge up
more blood.

strange casino
no clocks to
quell fear, we
do crosswords.

the odds of
three revised,
written down
to protect two.

now the pursuit
relentless as rivers
hidden in crooks
of your arms.

& we couldn't know
how desperately we

wanted you until

we couldn't

have you.

* * *

We had never discussed baby names, but it seems like we already know the answer. Every so often one of us will announce to the other something we do or don't like, mostly after we find out someone else is pregnant, as a means of warding off another breakdown. Every boy born during this period is called Leo for some reason. Meanwhile the girls alternate between mothballed names not popular since our grandparents' era: Edith, Vera, Poppy and Dorothy.

Did we have the conversation in London, when we were still new to each other and falling in love? Or was it when we first moved to Australia, setting off a cycle of unfortunate events—coronavirus, miscarriage, broken ankles—that marked one of the toughest years of Keren's life? We can't remember, but it doesn't really matter. In any event, it's always been there: Ray.

Especially for a girl; that's what we really both want, capped off with an 'e'. Elegant and arty, understated, sort of British but also very ocker, the antithesis of announcing her gender to the world via a backboard-shattering 4K Instagram video.

Rae haunts us for almost a year, unknown, unconfirmed and unreal. When we are not upset we discuss how we will dress her in ridiculous colours, play her 'Champagne

Supernova' by Oasis and 'Tender' by Blur as lullabies, and throw her into the waves as a toddler to make doubly sure she's a water baby.

Rae will be fearless, with her mother's constitution and her father's obsession with the new, an Art major who surfs barrels, a toddler who eats salmon and olives, then a kid who holds her own with the adults. She will be all hair because we are all hair, wild and beautiful, tanned skin and classically big eyebrows. Over this agonising interregnum we quietly manifest Rae into being, even as Keren's stubborn monthly spotting indicates the opposite.

Time drags on. The baby inevitably fails to materialise. Some of our friends fall pregnant for a second time, others who got together after us somehow pick the right numbers in the chaos Powerball of fertility. There are swollen bellies and swaddled men everywhere, parks rammed with prams, plans rearranged to make room for feeding schedules. Keren feels deficient, broken. She slumps around the house, head down, muttering about being cursed. My oldest friend and his fiancée manage to conceive in record time, and when he announces it to us with a surprisingly casual nonchalance, I'm so angry that I can't talk to him for a week. There is no resource for men locked into this situation, trapped in a halfway house between partner and father. We do all the tests, spend all the money we haven't made. The advice remains the same, vague and non-specific: keep trying and wait. I lose my temper at unrelated things, start exercising so frequently and aggressively that I injure my leg, then pull my shoulder at the gym. Replacing spiritual pain with physical agony seems like such a pathetic Psychology 101 move, but it works. When I am running I am not thinking. When I am lifting I am not worrying. It's just me, the repetitive motion and the same Linkin Park catalogue.

At the tail-end of their sophomore record *Meteora*, wedged between mega-hits 'Faint' and 'Numb', Chester and Mike go for the jugular on an esoteric number that references the music they wrote before they were famous. Its primary sample is a Japanese flute, the drums whip like chains against oil barrels, and with Shinoda on lead it's more mantra than melody. As I have done since I was a kid, I focus intensely on the lyrics as I stalk the streets, unable to find the right opening to talk to my wife about what this is also doing to me. They seem uncannily related to my current predicament.

I got a heart full of pain, head full of stress
Handful of anger held in my chest
Uphill struggle, blood, sweat, and tears
Nothing to gain, everything to fear

* * *

By the time the new year rolls around I have quietly revised my feelings around the name. I am thinking about legacy;

of Ray's attributes I want to crystallise and the others I really don't want to pass down. Pounding the pavement in battered, worn-out runners, I wonder if naming a new child after my mentally ill father is giving them a handicap before they've even exited the womb. I reflect on Marcell, my middle name, my paternal grandfather's name, our shared diagnoses. Forget delayed conception—such a loaded name could be the real curse. A girl would probably break the invisible cycle, I reason, but a boy? The prospect of naming my firstborn after Dad, once a given, suddenly seems terrifying. Two Marcells, two Rays. Four generations of this terror. I have read *Midnight's Children* and the magical realism of Gabriel García Márquez. There is definitely a strong case against pre-writing a person's fate into a sprawling family dynasty.

It is a philosophical predicament; both the right and wrong thing to do.

There is nobody I can properly discuss this hypothetical with. Not my siblings, probably secretly hoping I don't use the name at all, or Mum, who definitely doesn't need a constant reminder of her husband's death during her remaining years. It's awkward to explain why I am having an internal debate over the name of a child I'll likely be unable to have without serious medical intervention.

A few weeks later, a close friend's father—also a doctor— dies of suicide. The friend's wife is already in her second trimester with their second son. The entire thing spins me out, pulling out packed-in memories and forcing me to relive the experience. It's dredging up so much that it's clear I largely sleep-walked through it when it happened the first time. We are two sons who have known one another from the age of three, our fathers in the same line of work, both dying by their own hand far before retirement age. You can read into everything, but as a cornucopia of relatives close in on his house it feels more like a heavy book is belting me around the head. Defaulting to extreme caretaker mode, I draw my friend close and attempt to guide him through the siphoning out of emotion, the force field of impenetrability that helped me through to the other side. It clearly isn't necessary; with the benefit of a decade's social process, my friend approaches the situation in the opposite way to me. He tells everyone who will listen how his father died, how incomprehensible it is, what it is doing to him. In essence he never stops talking about it. Grief is sandwiched into every interaction. What took us five years seems to take him five hours.

It surprises nobody what they name the child.

I imagine what is going to happen when my non-son grows up to be like me, in a society more forgiving of mental illness but simultaneously more hostile to those who come of age making their mistakes in public. I consider the vast swathe of disasters that have sidestepped me because the online discourse was not yet in full swing when I was manic, revving up and out of control. Keren and I are having sex every day, rooting like rabbits month after month, and nothing is happening; there is no waking seasickness or skipped periods, and even though I'm not sure I want to name the child after him anymore, I can already see the caption when we announce the birth: 'Rae Seidler. Welcome back.'

Somewhere between January and June, after we find out another of our friends has fallen pregnant seemingly by accident, we have a particularly bad turn, and Keren and I eat pizza in the quiet of our locked-down apartment. I ask if we can start talking about it yet. She says she doesn't feel like it. No poetry will save me now.

* * *

July comes around again. The Delta variant is ripping through the country, so the only condoned form of socialising is that which happens while exercising. No strangers inside the house, nothing open except for takeout, everyone walking 20,000 steps a day while trying not to lose their minds. It is dramatically different, lonelier than I'm used to; it all feels like my tenth birthday party when nobody showed up. I don't want another bad July, so I schedule back-to-back one-on-one strolls and disappear for most of the morning.

By now I am used to having open discussions about our issues with conception. It's becoming clear that miscarriage still sits in that same darkly furnished room called Open

Secret where we used to keep depression, anxiety and suicide. I express doubt about us ever having kids of our own naturally, relay frustrations with the scientific community and fundamentally, a fear that Keren and I will fall out of love. I'm 34 now—roughly the age my father was when he had me. It's a yardstick I'm obsessed with, some sort of personal best that I'm not going to be able to achieve. For reasons I don't understand I'm deliberately setting myself up to fail against an expectation nobody actually ever had of me. Being a man has become synonymous with being frequently unimpressed with key parts of myself.

I've never felt closer to Dad in my life.

When I finally get back, Keren looks like she's seen an apparition. She hugs me and won't let go, the same way she did the morning I proposed to her. I ask her what the matter is and she sighs, summoning the stick from her jeans pocket.

The line on the plastic is thick and blue, so much clearer than before. I have read the instructions on the packaging so many times that I know it is irrefutable. And Keren's already done the calculations: it will be born the same month as Dad.

It would be lovely to say that this becomes a brilliant revelatory moment, but it's just another flicker that happens in our lives. One day it might be written down, or forgotten, but all that matters is right there and then: Keren and I, crying with relief in the kitchen, awkwardly slow dancing to the 'Baby on Board' playlist I made over a year ago but couldn't bear to listen to. Every song has the word 'baby' in the title even though it's totally contextually confused, like 'Be My Baby' by The Ronettes sliding into Britney's '. . . Baby One More Time' and Big Mountain's 'Baby I Love Your Way'. The whole thing is so bad it's funny, and as Mariah Carey belts out the final chorus of 'Always Be My Baby' the winter sun is flooding in through the north-facing window, covering the two of us pressed up against one another, looking at each other all misty-eyed, and for once, not seeing anything but the future.

EPILOGUE

To my daughter,

Welcome. There is much riding on your arrival, even if most of it is unspoken. We have not had a new member of our clan for nearly a quarter of a century. You will arrive at a family in stasis, where the arms between the branches of our tree have gnarled and hardened from disuse. You are the sunlight that brings us back to life, a reanimation I anticipate will take effect so suddenly that the first thing you see when you blink open those big, gorgeous eyes will be leaves curling around our fingers and wrists, hibiscus flowering from our mouths. Only with new soil can we truly begin to bury the old.

You are the first, as I was, as he was. The tide of love that rises to greet you will not go out for some time.

Despite this, I hope you will radiate heat, warmth and empathy for those who follow you or are not as lucky, as is your birthright. The joy that comes with being the sun that all other life moves around is also a responsibility. It is something I learned late but will try to instil in you early as we nurture and raise you from a tiny, twinkling bulb into whatever light source you choose to embody.

I am ready for you, but also disastrously unprepared, which I have been assured is normal: that nobody has it down, not even the second, third or fourth time. I was similarly not ready for the arrival of your mother, but this has proven to be the easiest and most satisfying subdivision of self; the positive charges that run through my system greatly outweigh insignificant negatives. I am not ready for you, but even I can admit that lately I have made exceptionally good decisions, decisions that are now amplified infinitely by the half of myself I have traded for your mother, a woman who seemingly runs off kinetic energy, tossing off sparkles as she moves through life.

Your inception was the most deliberate of decisions we have made together, two halves splitting themselves again to make space in a life that already feels whole.

I appreciate that though there are many light sources in this universe, we can only focus in on one at any given time. My interior self that sits and writes you letters in this cafe may go dormant for a time, as may fine dining, late night concerts and sex.

I cannot promise you, from the safe vantage point of nine hours sleep, that I will not find this reorientation difficult. But I know how solar power works. The rays that will envelop me simply by being in your presence will nourish and charge me up, sustaining me for many years. Even if drained in the short term, I will never be empty.

Stars in the sky and sun combined,

I cannot wait for you to light up our life.

J xx

ACKNOWLEDGEMENTS

I've spent my life poring over the acknowledgement sections of my favourite books, wondering what it would be like to ever write my own. Please excuse my excitement, it still amazes me that this moment has arrived at all.

Kelly, I'm so glad our paths crossed again at the perfect time. Thanks for pushing so hard for this book and understanding what it is truly about where many others fell short. I feel so safe with you and the entire A&U team and look forward to many more Potts Point lunches talking literature together.

Grace, you used the word so much during our pitch meetings it became a meme, but ultimately it encapsulates everything about you: you truly are transcendental. I am so appreciative of your unbridled and almost unhinged enthusiasm for this work. More than an agent, you're a wonderful friend and confidante. I cannot wait to work with you again.

Justin Wolfers, you absolute legend. I've been told by various employers that I'm not great at taking feedback, but I will happily take your notes any day of the week. You were the first to believe in this book and kept it on course even when I thought I'd lost hope. I am indebted to your guidance and compassion.

Tom and Sam, thanks for poring over every line and figuring out how to bring out the best in a manuscript in such record time. I feel smarter for having worked with you.

The early readers: Natalie Reiss, Lucy Howard-Taylor, Felix Chemke-Dreyfus, Hazel Michell, Hannah Nolan, Colin Ho and Vera Tate. You are all very dear to me. Special thanks also to Madeleine Gottlieb, who found the true core of this book and convinced me to pursue it, throwing away the rest.

Kate Steinweg, for always taking my calls and setting me straight.

My rambunctious, incredible family. People often remark on how unique our bond is and writing this book helped remind me of this. I love you all so much, you loud, overachieving bunch of misfits. Thank you for trusting me and allowing me to tell this story.

Violet Cafe in Hackney and La Piadina in North Bondi. Cafes are where the magic happens for writers. Thanks for letting me sit on one macchiato for two hours, staring out the window and scribbling away.

To the purveyors of loud, cathartic music. I will list you all because you deserve it: Dave Grohl, Hayley Williams, Josh Homme, Chris Cornell, Daniel Johns, Keith Flint, Ella Hooper, Sarah McLeod, Trent Reznor, Taylor Hawkins, Phil Jamieson, Yannis Philippakis, Serj Tankian, Matt Bellamy, Dexter Holland, Zack De La Rocha, Brody Dalle, Brandon Boyd, Mike Patton, Kele Okereke, Jon Toogood, Justin Hawkins, Ellie Rosewell, Jonathan Davis, Simon Neil, Karina Utomo, Anthony Kiedis, Gerard Way, Perry Farrell, Maynard Keenan and yes, Fred Durst. I owe you my identity, multiple careers and my life. I realise now more than ever that art is an expression of the purest sense of one's soul. Thank you for so selflessly sharing yours with me.

Chester Bennington. I really hope you and Ray are hanging out together in the next life. You are both the most endlessly giving people I ever encountered on this Earth.

Linkin Park. A band with your emotional insight and impact only comes along once in a generation. I'm glad I was there to witness it.

Mum. I'm in awe of who you are and what you've become in the face of unspeakable tragedy. This book, ultimately, is a testament to you.

Keren. It takes a certain kind of partner to let their husband disappear for hours at a time during lockdown to write—while still in the same room. You have been my champion for this incredibly taxing project, as you are for everything I do. I love you ridiculously.

Rae. One day you will read a faded old copy of this book and wonder what the fuss was all about. For now, I am thrilled to have manifested a daughter who looks almost exactly as I pictured her in my dreams.

Ray. Sorry for all the swearing.

A NOTE ON LYRICS

With grateful acknowledgement to the artists who wrote the songs quoted in this book:

p. 8—'See You Again' (feat. Charlie Puth), from *Furious 7: Original Motion Picture Soundtrack*, performed by Charlie Puth, Wiz Khalifa, written by Andrew Cedar, Cameron Thomaz, Charlie Puth, Dann Hume, Joshua Karl, Simon Hardy and Phoebe Cockburn, Atlantic Records, 2015.

pp. 19–20—'Evil', from *Antics*, performed by Interpol, written by Carlos Dengler, Daniel Kessle, Paul Banks and Samuel Fogarino, Matador, 2005.

p. 65—'XO Tour Llif3', from *Luv Is Rage 2*, performed by Lil Uzi Vert, written by Bryan Simmons and Lil Uzi Vert, Generation Now/Atlantic, 2017.

p. 69—'Papercut', from *Hybrid Theory*, performed by Linkin Park, written by Bradford Delson, Chester Bennington, David Farrell, Joseph Hahn, Michael Shinoda and Robert Bourdon, Warner Records, 2000.

p. 85—'My Generation', from *Chocolate Starfish and the Hot Dog Flavored Water*, performed by Limp Bizkit, written by Fred Durst, John Otto, Leor Dimant, Samuel Rivers and Wes Borland, Interscope, 2000.

p. 87—'One Step Closer', from *Hybrid Theory*, performed by Linkin Park, written by Bradford Delson, Chester Bennington, Joseph Hahn, Michael Shinoda and Robert Bourdon, Warner Records, 2000.

p. 87—'Break Stuff', from *Significant Other*, performed by Limp Bizkit, written by Brendan O'Brien, Fred Durst, John Otto, Leor Dimant, Sam Rivers and Wes Borland, Interscope, 2000.

pp. 75, 81—'Lean on Me', from *Still Bill*, performed by Bill Withers, written by Bill Withers, Columbia/Legacy, 1972.

p. 232—'Nobody's Listening', from *Meteora*, performed by Linkin Park, written by Bradford Delson, Chester Bennington, David Farrell, Joseph Hahn, Michael Shinoda and Robert Bourdon, Warner Records, 2003.

SUPPORT AND RESOURCES

This book was written from the vantage point of ten years since the suicide of my father and fifteen years since my own diagnosis. I have been blessed to have a supportive family and network of friends, not to mention access to psychological and psychiatric services, GPs and medication.

Suicide remains a massive problem for men in Australia, especially young ones like me. We make up an average seven out of every nine suicides every single day in Australia. In another life, I might not have been so lucky.

If any of the subject matter in this book has triggered difficult feelings for you, or made you realise that you may need help, please seek it out using the resources below or by talking with those close to you. There is always someone ready to listen.

Lifeline

Call 13 11 14

Available 24/7

Crisis support and suicide prevention services.

Suicide Call Back Service

Call 1300 659 467

Available 24/7

If you or someone you know is thinking about suicide, call this helpline for support.

Beyond Blue Support Service

Call 1300 22 4636

Available 24/7

Call for advice, referral and support from a trained mental health professional.

SANE Australia

Visit lifeline.saneforums.org

Safe, anonymous mental health discussion online, moderated 24/7 by mental health professionals.

Men's Line Australia

Call 1300 78 99 78

A telephone and online support, referral and information service, helping men deal with relationship problems in a practical way.

Jonathan Seidler is a writer, creative and culture critic. His work has been published frequently in *The Guardian*, *Sydney Morning Herald*, *The Australian*, *Monocle* and *GQ*. Jonathan co-founded long-running music website *One A Day*, launched two nationally syndicated fiction series for *Broadsheet* and recently commissioned, edited and published an Unyoked anthology of nature writing. As a creative director, Jonathan produced nationally recognised pro bono campaigns for Keep Sydney Open, One Wave and the Equality Campaign. He is a regular guest on ABC Radio National's *Download This Show*, discussing media, culture and technology. He once played drums in bands, now mostly in his garage.